BUILDING ME
WHILE I'M
BUILDING IT

8 Internal Attributes To Help You
Achieve External Results

Building Me While I'm Building It: Eight Internal Attributes to Help You Achieve External Results

Copyright © 2023 by Nesbitt Global Publishing

All rights reserved.

No portion of this book may be reproduced in any form without written permission from the publisher or author, except as permitted by U.S. copyright law.

This publication is designed to provide accurate and authoritative information in regard to the subject matter covered. It is sold with the understanding that neither the author(s) nor the publisher is engaged in rendering legal, investment, professional counseling, or other professional services. While the publisher and author(s) have used their best efforts in preparing this book, they make no representations or warranties with respect to the accuracy or completeness of the contents of this book and specifically disclaim any implied warranties of merchantability or fitness for a particular purpose. No warranty may be created or extended by sales representatives or written sales materials. The advice and strategies contained herein may not be suitable for your situation. You should consult with a professional when appropriate. Neither the publisher nor the author(s) shall be liable for any loss of profit or any other commercial damages, including but not limited to special, incidental, consequential, personal, or other damages.

Edited by Sinyon Ducksworth (www.letthepaperspeak.com)

Designed by C. Christopher Scott

Unless otherwise indicated, all Scripture quotations are taken from the King James Version of the Bible.

Scripture quotations marked ISV are from Copyright © 1995-2014 by ISV Foundation. ALL RIGHTS RESERVED INTERNATIONALLY. Used by permission of Davidson Press, LLC.

Scripture quotations marked ERV are from Copyright © 2006 by Bible League International

Scripture quotations marked AMP are from AMP Copyright © 2015 by The Lockman Foundation, La Habra, CA 90631. All rights reserved.

COPYRIGHT

Scripture quotations marked CEV are from Copyright © 1995 by American Bible Society For more information about CEV, visit www.bibles.com and www.cev.bible.

Scripture quotations marked GNT are from Good News Translation® (Today's English Version, Second Edition) © 1992 American Bible Society. All rights reserved. For more information about GNT, visit www.bibles.com and www.gnt.bible.

Scripture quotations marked MSG are from *The Message*. Copyright © 1993, 1994, 1995, 1996, 2000, 2001, 2002 by NavPress Publishing Group. All rights reserved. Used by permission.

Scripture quotations marked NIV are from Holy Bible, New International Version®, NIV® Copyright ©1973, 1978, 1984, 2011 by Biblica, Inc.® Used by permission. All rights reserved worldwide.

Scripture quotations marked NKJV are taken from the New King James Version®. Copyright © 1982 by Thomas Nelson. Used by permission. All rights reserved.

Scripture quotations marked NLT are from the Holy Bible, New Living Translation, copyright © 1996, 2004, 2015 by Tyndale House Foundation. Used by permission of Tyndale House Publishers, Inc., Carol Stream, Illinois 60188. All rights reserved.

Scripture quotations marked TPT are from The Passion Translation®. Copyright © 2017, 2018, 2020 by Passion & Fire Ministries, Inc. Used by permission. All rights reserved. ThePassionTranslation.com.

Scripture quotations marked ESV are from The Holy Bible, English Standard Version. ESV® Text Edition: 2016. Copyright © 2001 by Crossway Bibles, a publishing ministry of Good News Publishers.

ISBN: 978-1-7376705-5-1

1st edition, 2023

Printed in the United States of America

Contents

Introduction	VII
1. Building in Vision by Cedric Nesbitt	1
2. Building in Peace by Maria Mwangi	16
3. Building in Confidence by Char-Michelle McDowell	26
4. Building in Humility by Jaquay Reed	36
5. Building in Belief by Shyla Bassey	48
6. Building in Influence by Robin K. Butler	57
7. Building in Expansion by Tiffany Hodgest	69
8. Building in Excellence by Dr. Ansonya L. Pace-Burke	78
Affirmations for Your Journey	95

About the Authors	97
Sources Noted	107

Introduction

by Char-Michelle McDowell

Millions of people have dreams, but only 2% will actualize them. A few reasons for this include fear of the unknown, insecurities, feelings of inadequacy, and a lack of confidence. Having this kind of root system in our lives can imprison us; never stepping into our architectural nature. We are made in the likeness of God, to create and build what He's chosen us to produce.

This book is designed to encourage, empower and enrich the life of every creator and/or builder. These pages are filled with eight qualities that are essential for life. These inner qualities are meant to ignite, inspire and influence you to move from idea to impact; from dream to manifestation.

Building something of value takes work! You have to learn to push past your fears, rejection, perfectionism, validation, unhealthy comparisons, and those internal and external critics. Your unique gifts, talents, skills, and abilities are too valuable to be wasted. Your difference is what makes the difference. So, get ready to embrace the builder's mindset and embody its

DNA. Allow the words on each page to revive and refresh your perspective.

NOW LET'S GO BUILD!

Chapter 1

Building in Vision

by Cedric Nesbitt

Have you ever sat and pondered whether there was a difference between sight and vision? And if so, what distinguished the two?

As I was in pursuit of a deeper truth, I performed a Google search. That search led me to many optometry sites where sight and vision were discussed extensively. After exploring site after site, I gathered a simple medical truth—that *sight* has to do with seeing what you're looking at, and *vision* has to do with making sense of what you're seeing, where it is, and how to respond to it.

A person that has good vision is an individual whose eyes are functioning in sync, which optometrists refer to as "binocularity." While we may not use the word *binocularity* on an everyday basis, it does make us think of another related word that we may hear or even use occasionally. Are you able to guess what this word is?

Here's a clue: it actually begins with the same root word *bino...*

Binoculars. You know the device that you would use when going to a football or baseball game and you wanted to see the game from a far distance. Or if you're going out for a nature walk and you want to be able to see various animals or plants at a far distance. The times that you would enlist this device's usage is when things are too far to look at with your natural eyes and you need a different set of eyes to see a thing more clearly. This device assists an individual to make sense of what ordinarily would not make sense at all.

Now I hope you don't think we're going to spend the rest of the chapter discussing binoculars. The real conversation that I want us to have is how to keep your head and heart clear when your sight is being obstructed by difficulty, negativity, trouble, bad reports, failure, etc. Can you *see* where we're going?

New Eyes, His Eyes

I'm not sure about you, but on any given week there's often so much that's in front of my eyes with daily responsibilities, daily news updates, and other daily demands. I can hardly focus or concentrate on what really matters. Other times, I can sense and even see various things in abstracts. But honestly, struggle to grasp what I am seeing more clearly, pinpoint it, and what needs to be done with it at that moment. Can you relate? Have you ever been in this position?

It's at critical crossroads like these that we need God to give us His vision. Similar to the binoculars that we were discussing earlier, God wants to partner with us to help make sense of what is beyond us.

"Without prophetic vision, people abandon restraint..." Proverbs 29:18 (ISV)

One amazing attribute about God is that He is omniscient, which means that He is not only familiar with your present circumstances but he's also fully knowledgeable about your past and the entirety of your future. That by itself is altogether amazing, don't you think?

To provide more clarity concerning the verse, the phrase "prophetic vision" is referring to a person being able to see an accurate forecast of the future. What it is saying is that a person that exists without an accurate forecast of the future will begin to live their life as if they don't have a future. Without a picture of the future, we'll lose motivation. Without a picture of the future, we'll lose hope. Without a picture of the future, we'll lose encouragement. Without a picture of the future, we'll lose stick-to-itiveness. Do you see now why it's so important to have vision and not just sight?

Vision is a function of seeing through God's eyes whereas sight is a function of seeing through our limited natural eyes. While vision is the reality of the success and fulfillment that has been solidified by God's purpose and plan for our lives, sight is determined by our external circumstances and our corresponding emotions. My friend, vision propels you forward whereas sight confines you to your past and the here and now.

Clear It Up

Let's be honest, this is a very necessary conversation as December 2019 marked the first case of the coronavirus in the United States, and ultimately the pandemic changed things forever. Since then, while cases have cleared up, immunizations have been provided and certain procedures have since been set in place to control the virus, in many ways its psychological and even physical effects are still affecting many individuals. Here are some areas of impact to consider:

- Impact on Personal Relationships
- Impact on Employment
- Impact on Physical and Mental Health
- Impact on Routines
- Impact on Finances

In no way am I suggesting that everything surrounding the pandemic was negative. However, I do believe that we can agree that we were thrust into a different way of living and that many people are still processing our new normal.

Like the pandemic, there are often situations, circumstances, societal issues, personal issues, and beyond that can obstruct our sight. But in those times, it's important to keep a clear vision. It isn't denying what you see; instead, it's the ability to see beyond what you see. What we're about to discuss here are not only those specific areas that are important to have vision, but also strategies of how to see your way through difficult times. Are you ready to dig in?

Vision of Yourself

I'm about to age myself here, but in years past I'd be traveling on out-of-town trips and the only way to gain a sense of accurate direction was to stop and ask someone or to preferably pull over at a gas station and pick up a map. I'm pretty sure by now some of you reading this have absolutely no clue what I'm talking about. Don't worry though I'm about to turn the corner into more contemporary times.

Times have now changed, and we all use what's called GPS to get from place to place. Whether it is on long trips out of town or just plugging in an address that may be around the corner, these days ending up in the right place has a great deal to do with a powered-up device and the new faithful GPS. Technically GPS stands for the Global Positioning System, but years ago while facilitating a leadership session I came up with a significant meaning for the acronym. I identified GPS as "Grasping Your Present Self." Like the device that helps us to locate where we are and assists us in navigating to where we want to be, our identity is the internal mechanism within our lives that functions in a similar way.

Here's a 'let's get real' question, "Do you have a clear **present** vision of yourself?" The truth of the matter is that life is filled with all kinds of turns, twists, adjustments, and transitions. A crucial part of navigating the vision is to make sure that you consistently get proper updates and verify that you're still on course. Getting a clear picture of yourself is making sure that your identity is secure. Your identity is who you are at your core. It's the collective of your core beliefs, values, and what you think and feel about yourself. Here is why it's so important:

- It shapes your personality

- Either build or breaks down confidence

- Harnesses your emotions

- It is the root of your actions

We live in a world where there are so many things that are competing for our attention. Modern technology affords us the privilege of being able to upload and download, practically having access to anything that we desire within a matter of seconds. In order to get clear about the vision of who we are many times we must untie ourselves from the rat race of life and quiet ourselves. When we take time to seek God, He alone will release the vision for our lives. That means getting the picture of how He sees us and adopting that picture as our everyday reality.

> "Jesus went to the area of Caesarea Philippi. He said to his followers, "Who do people say I am?" They answered, "Some people say you are John the Baptizer. Others say you are Elijah. And some say you are Jeremiah or one of the prophets." Then Jesus said to his followers, "And who do you say I am?" Simon Peter answered, "You are the Messiah, the Son of the living God." Jesus answered, "You are blessed, Simon son of Jonah. No one taught you that. My Father in heaven showed you who I am." Matthew 16:13-17 (ERV)

Please know the reason why it's so important to get God's vision for your life and a secure identity is that situations, society, and other people will always have their say so about who you are. While we cannot totally isolate ourselves from society or remove people and their opinions, we can control their impact on us. By setting in place a clear vision of who you are:

- You build your identity as your foundation.

- Seek to understand your experiences through the filter of self-identity. What the experience meant to you and taught you.

Vision of Your Past

I was talking to a friend the other day and we were discussing something that had taken place in college. It was such a life-giving conversation that put a smile on my face because it brought up great memories. As we took turns retelling the story, it began to feel like it all happened yesterday. After we got off the phone, I sat and thought about it further. What we were talking about actually happened over 25 years ago. It left me somewhat stunned because I couldn't believe that so much time had passed between that event and now. Who I was then and now.

In reality, there's nothing wrong with reminiscing about "the good old days." It can actually boost your mood and create a sense of gratitude. However, being stuck in the past is an entirely different story. Here's a very real question, "Do you have a clear vision of your past?"

At the moment, it was great having 'catch-up' conversation with my friend. But for me to continue beyond that conversation living in that previous state of being, would be another thing. We have all had a measure of the good, bad, and ugly that has happened in our lives, and I don't think anyone that has lived for a number of years can say anything different. But one thing I've witnessed, whether I take the time to speak with individuals one-on-one or facilitate workshops or conference events, it's the same question; "How do I truly move on from what's happened in my past?"

It could be that you're presently in or have previously experienced a failed relationship. Maybe you're having a very difficult time forgiving yourself for a mistake that you made, and you keep pushing the repeat button in your mind that not only replays the situation, but also what you could've done differently. It could also be that you're holding on to a limiting belief from childhood that doesn't serve you. Regardless of what the situation is, without proper vision of your past it can hold you back from being all that you can be and prevent you from enjoying the present moment.

Here are 7 Identifiers That You Are Stuck in The Past:

1. There is an unhealthy level of reminiscing about how things used to be, and you wish they were still the same and you could go back in time.

2. You constantly blame yourself and have a hard time moving on from past mistakes.

3. You keep reliving traumatic moments from the past.

4. You have no hopes, goals, or plans for the future.

5. You have regrets and wish that you had/could do things differently.

6. You are bitter and hold on to grudges.

7. You were conditioned into self-defeating behavior and low self-esteem as a child.

The truth of the matter is that it's impossible to bring adjustment to our vision of the past if we go on believing that there isn't anything that needs adjustment. Start with using the 7 signs above as markers that assist in identification.

> **"My friends, I don't feel I have already arrived. But I forget what is behind, and I struggle for what is ahead." Philippians 3:13 (CEV)**

I love the verse above because the writer keeps things on an even playing field. He doesn't speak of himself as someone that has already achieved success in this area and is looking down on those that he's speaking with. He actually refers to himself as someone that considers getting the vision of his past together, a work in progress. He goes on to provide a very healthy tool for aligning our vision of the past with where it needs to be by saying, "But I forget what is behind." I really believe the idea here is **not** to get amnesia and totally forget everything that has happened previous to the current moment in your life. More importantly, I believe the writer is trying to drive home the point that while the past is significant, it isn't superior. When the thought that says the best of your life is behind you, God wants us to know that He has better with your name on it in the future.

> **"You plotted evil against me, but God turned it into good, in order to preserve the lives of**

many people who are alive today because of what happened." Genesis 50:20 (GNT)

There are times when God will allow us to go through temporary pain so that we can be a permanent solution. In other words, your past is simply the down payment for all of the many amazing things that are about to happen in your life, but also through your life. In reading Genesis, we know Joseph went through a very extensive process where if anyone could have an inaccurate vision of their future it would be him. But after the dust settled and he fully assessed his past pain, Joseph made the above statement. There are a few things that he did let go of from the past so that he could move on:

- Let go of any and all grudges
- Practice gratitude
- Learn to live in the present

Vision of Your Future

"I know what I'm doing. I have it all planned out - plans to take care of you, not abandon you, plans to give you the future you hope for." Jeremiah 29:11 (MSG)

My wife and I have been married now going on 24 years. Every once in a while I'll say to her, "go ahead and put on something because I'm going to take you out tonight."

At the beginning of our relationship when I would say that, she would say things like, "Really?" and, "Where are we going?" Some twenty-plus years later she doesn't make statements or ask questions like that anymore, she simply takes action. Over the years I've proven myself that when I ask her to put on clothes and mention to her that we're about to go out, she knows that there are some exciting plans I have in store for that day or evening.

The verse above points to the fact that God is telling us to gear up and get ourselves together because He has plans for us. The reason that we question God's intent is if we're still getting to know Him and His track record, but to know Him is to understand that there are amazing plans He has in store. Let me go ahead and pause to make a statement. If you're reading this then it means that out of all the things that you have been through, **the reason why you're still here is that God has some amazing plans for you**.

You have more to look forward to than your past. You have more to look forward to than your present. There are amazing plans that God has for you in your future! Do you believe that? If you do, then it is of great importance that you begin to develop a healthy and accurate vision of the future.

Another translation of the same scripture mentioned above, Jeremiah 29:11 (NIV) reads,

"For I know the plans I have for you," declares the LORD, "plans to prosper you and not to harm you, plans to give you hope and a future."

In addition to the keywords "plans" and "future", the verse also mentions the word "hope." To fully understand what hope is, let's discuss what it is not.

- Hope Is Not Optimism
- Hope Is Not the Full Knowledge of a Thing
- Hope Is Not Possession of a Thing

Hope is usually necessary in not-so-favorable circumstances. It is the ability to "look on the bright side of things" and see challenges as opportunities. It is speaking things that are not as though they were. It is a confirmation within, that better days are approaching. It is your ability to encourage other people when you, too are going through "a rough patch." I like to say that hope is the expectation of a favorable future. Hope is one of the missing ingredients in the days that we live in.

Just to be super transparent, while writing this chapter I received a phone call that my father had passed away unexpectedly. At that moment, I really didn't know what to say or do. It was as if someone took their fist, punched me in my stomach, and knocked the wind out of me. I was completely devastated.

Not only was I in the middle of adding the finishing touches to this anthology, but my team and I were just a few weeks from hosting a conference in Texas. On top of all of the planning, teams ready to execute those plans, and the other many things happening at that moment, this news of my father dropping on me out of nowhere made me ask the question, "Should I even continue what I'm doing, or do I simply need to cancel everything?" After all, no one would have anything to say if they knew everything that was presently taking place. If anything, they would probably encourage me to cancel everything and insist that I reschedule it for another time so that I could handle what needed to be handled and mourn.

As I was just about to give into everything that was playing through my head and send out texts and phone calls to cancel that week's scheduled appointments and the conference as a whole; something that my father would say came up in my spirit. I immediately paused everything as I heard, "Keep going and do all that you can do, and what you can't do; don't do." That sound wisdom that I could always count on dad giving me when he was living, was coming up in my spirit even in his absence at a time that I needed it most.

Just then a peace came over me that took away the stress and even some of the sadness. It was at that moment that for the first time in my life, I really understood *hope*. I was fully aware of all of the things that were happening around me and to me, but also had a vision of the future that stood before me.

I wasn't hopeless. Despite it all, I had so many reasons to lift my head and live to see another day.

I can't even begin to imagine the difficult things that you've been through, and what it takes to be you. What I do know is that somehow with God's grace and your determination to continue on, you're still here. The challenge now is to get clarity of vision so that you can see what should've discontinued you only served to define you. Put it all under your feet my friend and dare to look at life now in this elevated place.

Chapter 2

Building in Peace

by Maria Mwangi

I am a mama bear at my core. *Mama Bear* means that I am a protector of all things that are mine and have no issue using my strength if needed to provide that protection. I will protect my cubs with all that I have. And I have learned to protect the peace in my life with that same *Mama Bear* mentality. But it wasn't always that way.

Six years ago at the age of forty, my healthy-looking husband, Ken, suffered a stroke. It was the first of May. By May 17th, he had passed on. He was a very hands-on wonderful daddy to our boys. My profession is in the event industry so I worked most weekends. You can easily say that Ken was the primary parent. So when I was left alone with seven and nine-year-old grieving boys, life changed in a big way for all of us.

We lived in San Antonio, Texas at the time. By July 1st, I had moved my boys and me back home to Arizona where my mom and a lot of my family lived so I could have support. My life seemed like a disaster zone. We lost the pillar of our family, our home, the boys changed schools. I left a job I absolutely loved.

I was well on my way to bankruptcy, drowning in medical bills. And we left so many people that we loved back in Texas.

The move back to Arizona felt like the best thing to do. I felt the need to be with my family as well as the church family that knew Ken well and would help mentor our boys. It was a whole lot to process. But I became so focused on the boys' mental health and trying to start this life all over again, that I lost myself. Truth is, I had no idea who I was without Ken. We were just a great team together. I did not know where he started and where I left off. How was I supposed to live without him? I felt incomplete. So, I filled the void with what everyone else wanted from me.

I said yes to boards I was previously on before we moved to Texas. I volunteered at the boys' school and I took all the contract jobs that came my way. I overbooked myself to stay busy. I was running from the feelings of grief, pain, and trauma. I was so busy being everything to everyone that my life became overwhelmingly chaotic. Then I succumbed to guilt and pressure that even if my plate was running over, and I was tormented inside with pain, I still needed to be serving in any capacity asked of me because it was 'for the Lord' by doing God's work in the church. I was like the rabbit in Alice in Wonderland that was always very late for very important dates. I started realizing that I was *busy* with everyone else's desires and was missing MY life!

My two boys, I call them my miracle babies, I was too busy to enjoy time with them because I did not know how to say *no*. Life was just going through the motions, existing and not living. I was exhausted, cranky, and my health was showing all the signs of pure burnout.

Before we had our boys, Ken and I were told I would not have children after losing our third pregnancy. We were thinking of adopting a baby from Kenya where Ken was from when we were finally blessed with our firstborn, Ethan, and then our baby, Andre, exactly two years later. The pregnancies were full of high risks, doctor visits, hospital stays, and the dreaded bed rest followed by emergency c-sections that almost took my life and the life of our babies. We wanted nothing more than to have these boys. And now here I was, a widow and missing out on *living* with my boys in my effort to avoid feeling my feelings.

For many years, wine had already been my go-to for relaxation and peace. When Ken's passing flipped our world, my already too many glasses of wine turned into a bottle or five without even realizing it. I told myself that I had every excuse to drink away my problems and I dared anyone to tell me to stop. Around the first anniversary of Ken's passing, I experienced a traumatic event involving my family. This sent me further into a downward spiral.

I did not think my life could get any lower than it was, but boy did it! My family that I moved back to Arizona for, the family that was everything to me was now divided. I am not talking about a few people here. I am Mexican. So we are talking about a lot of family members. My shattered heart broke into even more pieces when my son came to me crying that he had witnessed some abusive interactions and was confused about what he saw. I had to completely cut people out of my life that I never imagined would not be in it. I never felt so alone and lost. If it had not been for my children, I don't think I would have survived.

Two years into my grief journey and one-year post family trauma, I was living in full-on survivor mode where my goal was to just not drown in life and to provide for my kids the best way I knew how. My oldest came to me saying that he was sick of me drinking wine every night and that he was scared of me dying just like Daddy did. That was all it took. Sobriety was a choice that I made that night. I reached out to a friend that I knew who lived a sober lifestyle. She loved on me, told me what steps to follow, and took me to my first AA meeting.

I grew up in church. My parents were leaders in the church. So we were at church nine days a week if that says anything. But the moment I walked into that AA meeting and was so loved on by complete strangers, it gave me a sense of belonging that I had never felt. No judgment, no one pushed belief on me, told me that I was bad, sinful, or on the path to hell for my confessions of alcoholism. No one tried to make me feel guilty or told me that God *told them* that I should volunteer for something. *Get busy in ministry work. That will take your mind off living in sin.* Nope. They just wanted to help me succeed, that was it! My AA meetings became a safe haven that I truly enjoyed and continue to attend today.

As for my hectic, keep-busy lifestyle, I had tried to pull back and slow down several times over the years. However, the pushback and guilt from people would put me right back into my old people-pleasing ways. It all truly clicked for me when I was reading the *Eikonic Leadership* book by Dr. Ansonya L. Pace-Burke. She wrote "Good Stewardship is imperative to the eikonic leader's ability to shine and flourish. You have to be intentional about nurturing and guarding your unique and multifaceted gifts."[1] This was life changing for me! This gave me the permission to be me, live my life and protect my peace. I took the next steps she laid out as a road map to this new peace I had declared for my life. I am going to paraphrase the steps,[2] but you will need to read the amazing book for a deeper dive.

1. *Embrace* - She stated that when you don't embrace who you are, you don't live authentically. This hit me because I realized I was playing several roles like I was a character in a movie called *Maria's Life* versus living my authentic life. I was playing the role of daughter, wife, mom, friend, church member, and employee. Being who I thought everyone wanted me to be and not who I really was. Because I was not being my authentic self, I used alcohol for comfort. And it became a routine turned habit I relied on each night to wind down. I turned to it for peace versus creating my peace. The wine was helping me avoid feeling the feelings that would ultimately help me find the peace my soul was searching for.

2. *Affirm* - Daily positive affirmations. My go-to for affirmations is the book, *Live to WIN, 5 Essentials for our Victory and Success* by Evangeline Colbert.[3] The book has a chapter of winning words and victory verses that are part of my daily routine. I also have a printout that I got in church years ago called the "40 I AM's" that I have on my desk at work. I also have an app that sends me several affirmations a day.

3. *Set Boundaries* - MAN, OH MAN was this one hard! I was so scared to say the word NO. When I realized that saying *No* was an actual sentence and I did not have to make excuses or explain my *No*, that gave me such power over my life again. I was raised that saying no to parents or family members was disrespectful and you just did what they were requiring of you because no matter what, family is family. Choosing to protect my peace was not popular and some saw me as selfish and were bold enough to tell me so. I have learned to say "I am sorry that I am not providing you with what you are expecting from me, but this is what I am mentally capable of providing for you at this time." Some relationships changed or went away altogether. I would be lying if I said that it did not hurt. I was shocked at some reactions but I had to trust that God was removing relationships that were not benefiting my life and my peace.

4. *Care* - Dr. Burke asked the question "When was the

last time you felt rested and not overworked?" I had to put the book down and have a good cry. She went on to say, "you are neglecting yourself and headed straight for burnout or a blowup. You must take care of yourself to excel and thrive. Rest is a gift and a blessing from God for which you are Eligible." This last sentence shook my soul, *rest was a gift that I am eligible to use*, I questioned. Why didn't anyone tell me this? I was taught that rest was being lazy. I literally had to learn how to relax and enjoy life even though my To-do list was not complete and my house was a mess. I also had to learn to allow my children to rest and not inflict the same standards onto them that I grew up with. I never knew what a chill day was, like where you lay around and watch tv, take naps, or just talk with friends. I couldn't sit on the couch until the carpet was pattern vacuumed, the floors were moped, I had a load in the dishwasher, a load of laundry going, and the crockpot cooking. *How many precious hours cuddling on the couch with my late husband did I miss out on because of this?*—I pondered. I am not encouraging you to not keep up with your house. I am just saying it does not have to be perfect all the time.

Without rest and peace, I could not shine or flourish. I could not begin to know who I was and what I wanted to even begin building the life I desired for myself. So once I felt peace, I wanted nothing more than to protect it and keep it in my life. It was like quenching a thirst I had. All of a sudden my life ran smoother and was more fulfilling. I began making my moves with *purpose*. The decision to live protecting my peace did not bid well with some friends, family, my job, and church members. I did learn that if God did not *tell ME* that I was to take on a new task, he wasn't going to tell everyone else what I should be doing and leave me clueless.

I still overcommit at times or take a quick shower versus the long hot bath that I know my body needs. But, I am conscious of the lack of balance and do my best to make the necessary moves to course-correct. If I am determined to reach a goal, I may not realize that my stride in life has turned into full-on race mode. I have accountability partners that have permission to speak into my life to help me pull back the reins. *Building* is more of a process, not something we should race through. This is when you lose control in the middle of the building and lose your peace as well.

I am now going on four years sober. I am very proud of myself. I had to admit a lot of things about myself and that was very hard to do, but I am a better person for it. I live my life intentionally, authentically, and with *purpose* now. I would rather regret not doing something or trying something new versus having not tried at all. Some of my ideas are brilliant and some have blown up in my face. I have learned from the wins and I am blessed for the lessons of my failures. I live life with no regrets.

I have enjoyed forming new relationships and learned to let them go when I noticed signs that my peace was at risk. My home and soul being at peace is a priority I am no longer willing to compromise. I've also learned how to reflect and connect. You see, I've let my guard down forming new relationships. However, when I saw the flags, I justified them. My soul was not at peace but my heart was...full speed ahead! By reflecting and connecting with my inner self, I pinpointed my wanting to feel what I had with Ken again so badly.

As I reflected, I came to the conclusion that what I had with Ken was not just a marriage. He was my soulmate. We blended in an imperfect way that was made perfect for us. I believe that I will love again, but I will never have what I had with Ken. I've had to come to terms with that before I even try to forge something new with another. He is gone but our love will live forever in my heart. We have two beautiful boys that are a reflection of our love. Coming to that realization caused me to start a new grief journey.

My boys and I are having a good time together, *living*. We are truly enjoying each other and are savoring our moments before my oldest is off to college in two years. We realized that although my late husband's possessions are reminders of him, he is really in the stories and memories that we laugh about together. We say his phrases, go to his favorite places to eat, and try to maintain a balance of keeping his memory alive and feeling the feelings, as we make new memories together.

We visit the sadness of his loss, and give our grief its space, but we do our best to not live in the sad place. Sometimes the tears flow for no particular reason. I no longer think my tears are weakness. They are healing. They are peace. So, I no longer apologize for them. Our job is to live and enjoy life, like he would want us to. My teenage boys and I now say the *I love you's* freely. We talk openly without judgment, spend money on concert tickets, and sometimes just fly by the seat of our pants when we leave the house for the day. Life is short. We live it and enjoy it to the fullest!

With God guiding me, I am no longer playing any roles in an inauthentic life. I am now directing my life as the main character who feels the feelings, good or bad. This brings me peace. I am the woman who now owns her mistakes, apologizes when wrong, loves like our lives depend on it, and lives without fear of the future. "Take one! Take Two! TAKE ME"

> *"Start over, my darling, Be brave enough to find the life you want and courageous enough to chase it. Then start over and love yourself the way you were always meant to"* - *Madalyn Beck*

Chapter 3

Building in Confidence

by Char-Michelle McDowell

The American writer and lecturer of self-improvement, Dale Carnegie said, *"Inaction breeds doubt and fear. Action breeds confidence and courage. If you want to conquer fear, do not sit home and think about it. Go out and get busy."*[4]

Millions of people have great dreams within their hearts, but only 2% will actualize those dreams.[5] As a creative and builder, this statistic should concern you. It should cause you to ask the question, "What is hindering people from making their dreams a reality?" Then, if you are a reflective person like me, it should make you ask yourself, "What is hindering **ME** from moving forward and actualizing my dreams?"

Think about that for a moment and journal your thoughts. Is fear hindering you? Is it insecurities? Are you looking for moral support from specific individuals and not getting it? Do you feel you need more resources until you can take action? Are you waiting for someone else's approval or permission? Lastly, do you lack confidence? If you can identify with any of these, guess what? You are not alone!

For 13 years, I was imprisoned by the spirit of rejection, which resulted in me being insecure and having a lack of confidence. Although I was born into a loving, fun, and Christian family, I somehow still felt devalued, and it just didn't make sense. I often asked, "Lord, why do I feel this way? Why is this emptiness in my soul? I am loved by so many and made plenty of friends, but why still this hole in my soul?"

After much prayer and constant reflection, I realized that I was different. I simply didn't fit in. As a person who didn't fit in, I often looked to others for approval. I was thirsty for someone to affirm me and the purpose for which I believed I was called and chosen. Expecting others' approval of me, only left me hurt to my core and very disappointed. It wasn't until I became an adult that I began to pray and ask God, "Why am I so insecure and why do I lack confidence?"

After much prayer, I was led to read books such as *Approval Addiction* and *The Root of Rejection*. Both of these books are by Joyce Meyers and I highly recommend them. Through these books, God shed light that I had a root of rejection. I came to understand there was a spiritual seed that was planted in my life because of life's happenings and experiences. This seed had taken root and the fruit of it definitely showed up in my life. Let's talk about the power of a seed for a moment.

Power of a Seed

Seeds are potent and when planted deeply, they will surely develop roots so they can eventually produce fruit (results).

For example, if I plant an apple seed, it will take root and its tree will eventually produce apples as the fruit. In like manner, the devil, our enemy, intentionally plants evil seeds like rejection so our tree will bear the fruit of things such as– *depression, lack of confidence, sadness, loneliness, insecurity, inadequacy, timidity, and the fear of rejection or even self-rejection.*

One of the reasons we cease to build is because we are bound. The enemy wants to make you feel, think, and believe there is something wrong with you, when in fact there isn't. This type of thinking simply causes you to perform and pretend in front of others, instead of being your authentic self, confidently. Anytime there is an open door in our lives, the enemy can access it and begin to build strongholds to keep us bound.

You see, as long as the devil finds an opening or access point in our lives, he will take advantage. I grew up without my biological dad, who was in the Navy, and died when I was one. This affected me growing up and I looked for love in all the wrong places. When a mother or father is absent from a child's life, this can cause a child to feel unwanted, unloved, or even abandoned. Whether we realize it or not, this situation becomes an open door in a child's life. From a spiritual perspective, a seed of rejection is planted in a person's life/heart, causing them to succumb to the feelings previously mentioned.

Although I was loved by my family and grew up in a good environment, I still looked to be loved and affirmed. I now know that affirmation is my love language, and fathers are wired to give identity and affirmation to their kids. I was missing that part of my life, and as a result, was insecure. But I'm free now! When you find yourself still dealing with these types of symptoms, know that it's time to uproot the root, so you can bear the right fruit!

An improper root system will hinder you from building what God has placed in your heart to build with excellence. It is time for you to live your dreams and leave your mark. Allow your works to live beyond you, creating a legacy that blooms because of a powerful seed called *confidence*.

What is Confidence?

When I talk about confidence, I am not talking about having an arrogant or egotistical spirit. The confidence I want to encourage you starts with God. Without a relationship and intimacy with God, pure confidence doesn't exist, however, self-reliance does. It's never God the Father's intention for us to rely on ourselves to do the things He has chosen us to do. He wants you and me to depend on Him solely, as this brings Him glory. The reason I believe in myself is not that I'm so great, but because of the greater One (Holy Spirit) who lives on the inside of me, which gives me the ability to greatly produce.

> *"Ye are of God, little children, and have overcome them: because greater is he that is in you, than he that is in the world."* – 1 John 4:4 (KJV)

Through Christ Jesus, we have the ability to step into the victory that's already won over rejection, insecurity, lack of confidence, and much more!

According to the Merriam-Webster dictionary[6], confidence is 1) the state of feeling certain about the truth of something, 2) a feeling of self-assurance, arising from one's appreciation of one's own abilities or qualities, and 3) consciousness of one's powers. I love the study of words and learned that confidence is of Latin origin meaning **"have full trust."** Whew! That's a mouth full! But let's pause here to ask a quick question. Do you have **FULL** trust or belief that you can build and actualize your vision and dreams? Think about that for a second and be honest with yourself.

Now, I can be honest with you. I have learned and continue to learn that having full trust or belief that I CAN is a continuous process. I constantly meditate on and remind myself what God spoke concerning me and the skills, talents, and gifts I possess. In studying the Bible, I learned something and I know it's a master key that can unlock you from the imprisonment of a lack of confidence and all other deficiencies attached to it. Listen closely. When God speaks to you about doing or building something, that is your confirmation that you have exactly what it takes to do it, build it, and be it! Here are a few examples to help support my perspective.

- According to Genesis 6, God was grieved that He had made mankind on the earth. There was much corruption, but Noah was found righteous. God was going to send a flood, therefore, God told Noah to build an ark. It had never rained before, but we do not see in scripture where Noah doubted himself regarding building the ark. He obeyed God and his family was saved from the flood just as God promised.

- According to Judges 6, the children of Israel were oppressed by their enemy because of sin. God chose Gideon, a mighty warrior, to save them by going to war, but he started giving excuses. He confessed that he was the least of his family and that his clan was the weakest link. He also asked God for three confirmations regarding this task. Finally, Gideon obeyed and went to war, and Israel was saved from their enemies as promised.

- According to Luke 1:26-38, an angel of the Lord came to a virgin girl named Mary, who was engaged to Joseph. He told her that she is going to bear the Son of God, he will be great, and his name shall be called Jesus. Mary asked one question because she couldn't naturally comprehend how this would be. After the angel explained that the Holy Spirit will overshadow her, she responded, "be it unto me."[4]

Each of these persons responded differently, but in the end, they still obeyed God. They had FULL confidence, not in themselves, but in what God said. It is that truth that gives you the hope and courage to follow through with confidence. How have you been responding in times past? Were you like

Gideon, having feelings of inadequacy and thinking of yourself as less than? Or perhaps you were like Mary and Noah, asked few questions, and obeyed. In either case, I think you get my point.

Please know that I'm not saying we do not need confirmation sometimes because we do, but ultimately the goal is to know and have full trust that you have the skills, talents, and gifts to do what God is asking of you. Having this understanding will definitely cause your future responses to be different.

Do you feel the chains breaking and those root systems being uprooted? You have just been untied and unlocked from those things that kept you stale, stagnant, and stuck! Your potential can now be unleashed so you can fulfill your destiny.

In this next season of your life, trust yourself fully. Be confident and certain when God calls you to do or build something. Believe you are already capable and you have the goods. Now that you understand the meaning of confidence, let's discuss how to cultivate and embrace this internal quality, so you can experience its benefits.

Cultivating & Embracing Confidence

Confidence is an internal quality that has to be cultivated or developed from the inside out, not the outside in. Today, our modern world is filled with social media outlets where many have grown accustomed to receiving external affirmations, which only build a temporary kind of confidence. This unstable self-assurance is mainly aroused by the number of likes and hearts received by one's social media friends. To nurture confidence, one must put in the work and first discover purpose (the reason you exist).

Purpose can be realized in various ways. One way is by asking yourself, "what problem do I love to solve? What do people often request of me?" These may sound basic, but doing a little bit of self-coaching has tremendous outcomes. You realize why you were born, which then connects to your identity. Being sure of these two things, causes you to easily weed out the seeds that don't belong in your life and cultivate the confidence that does belong. I encourage you to boost your confidence and develop it by doing the following:

1. Spend time with God and cut those bad roots by uprooting and denouncing them in prayer.

2. Make a list of the skills, gifts, and abilities you've used to serve others. This creates a conscious awareness of your superpowers and brings clarity to what you possess!

3. Find and memorize scriptures like Deuteronomy 31:6 (NLT), "So be strong and courageous! Do not be afraid and do not panic before them. For the Lord your God will personally go ahead of you. He will neither fail you nor abandon you."

4. Meditate on the Word daily so you can have good success.[5]

Cultivating takes time, so give yourself some grace and trust the process of gaining and building your confidence.

In my first book, *Just B.E.E. IT*, I talk about the difference between two concepts: *accept versus embrace*.[9] To accept something is simply to receive it. Although embracing includes accepting, it just goes a little bit deeper. For example, I can accept God's plan for my life, but not like it. In turn, this means my heart isn't truly connected to His purpose and plans for my life. When you embrace a thing, your heart posture shifts. You begin to take ownership, and your strut and speech are different to the point where others notice and respect it.

Since gaining internal clarity from God about my identity and purpose, any external whispers or affirmations should be confirmation of what I've gained internally. If it doesn't match, then I have a right to guard it from my heart and reject it. So do you! Never second guess what you know God has spoken to you about you. Be Confident! We all must realize that CONFIDENCE is a powerful quality that has many benefits and its imprint leaves a great impact.

Benefits and Impacts of Confidence

As human beings, we want to know what's in it for us! You may be wondering, what's the benefit of having confidence? First, having confidence causes you to be your authentic self. You will truly shine through and you don't have to pretend to be something or someone you're not. Second, your relationships will improve because you're not comparing yourself to others, or thinking about what others think of you. Lastly, having increased confidence allows you to break the cycle of overthinking and quieting the inner critic.[10]

As you build, value these benefits because it causes you to focus; prohibiting you from giving your attention to all internal and external critics. Set your mind and know that you have what it takes to build and rebuild again. Your impact shall be great!

When you walk in confidence your impact on others will be effortless. You will speak and people will listen. They will take action because they trust you and recognize you have their solution in your mouth. My friend, don't be afraid! Celebrate and be excited about your authenticity and leave your mark in the earth for generations to come. Go and build with the confidence you now possess!

Chapter 4

Building in Humility

by Jaquay Reed

What a journey life has been from childhood into adulthood. Learning right from wrong, knowing what is good and not. My biggest struggle was learning that there are times in life when I must surrender myself, my way of thinking, and be clothed in a spirit of humility. Making it all about me, myself, and I was a form of pride that was unrealized until different life lessons taught me to cultivate a sense of humility that has forever changed my life, kicking pride out the door of my heart.

Making mistakes used to be hard for me to accept. *Do you always have to be right?*—I'd question myself. And a resounding, *Yes*, always followed.

Depending on the conversation and/or the person, I was always right in my mind. Everything needed to be perfect. Well in my late twenties, spiritual convictions came and tore all of that down. I began to understand that mistakes are inevitable, and I would make some in order to grow in life. Accepting that I am not always right was not hard but refreshingly easy. In conjunction, I had to also accept that I am not perfect, only human. My way of *right* living could only be made perfect through submission to Jesus Christ (Romans 5:1, TPT). Interesting thing is that I got saved at the age of thirteen but learned this truth close to age thirty when I began to learn about humility.

Humility...what does that mean? Merriam-Webster dictionary definition - "Freedom from pride or arrogance: the quality or state of being humble." Another definition is, "A modest or low view of one's own importance; humbleness," from the Oxford Languages dictionary. These definitions appear to match Philippians 2:3 *(see these versions NLT/TPT)*.

> "Be free from pride-filled opinions, for they will only harm your cherished unity." (The Passion Translation, TPT)

So, humility results in freedom from pride, which leads to other benefits. The promise of grace is another benefit. According to *1 Peter 5:5, AMP* "*...and all of you, clothe yourselves in humility toward one another [tie on the servant's apron], for God is opposed to the proud [the disdainful, the presumptuous, and He defeats them], but He gives grace to the humble.*" I have been on a journey of praying to be "clothed" in humility, and grace is supplied every time. I have also noticed I am more intentional about being accountable for my actions. Selflessness takes over when I would normally be selfish. In what could be confrontational situations, I find myself responding constructively and not reacting defensively. Through humility, I find it effortless to forgive. The one benefit of walking in humility that I want to expound on is *spiritual breakthrough.*

I am going to share the most recent spiritual breakthrough I experienced while practicing walking in humility. From my teenage years in the 90s until recently in 2021, my mom and I would 'bump heads'. There were confrontations between the two of us that would be very sporadic, and I could never understand it.

I was born and raised in Chicago, IL and in 2014 I relocated to Phoenix, AZ. Along with all the wonderful things that were happening in my life, I thought the distance would be the ending factor for the head bumping between my mom and me. Well, I was a thousand percent wrong. A few months after I moved to Phoenix, I had to go back to Chicago because my dad was expected to get a heart transplant. During that visit, a confrontation occurred.

What was supposed to be a joyous celebratory time of the healing miracle Jesus had performed in giving my dad a new heart, this cloud of confusion came about and left casting shadows of dismay. I remember being in the hospital room, so overjoyed with my dad and mom in conversations. Then things turned after my mom made a statement about having grandchildren through me and my sister. In the past, I had explained that I was waiting on the Lord for my husband and children. But nevertheless, this desire of hers resurfaced.

In response to her comment, I said something to the effect of: "I sure hope that's God's plan for me because if I not, I feel sorry for you."

I did not say this spitefully nor intended for it to be. It was an assertion of my peace in knowing my life is in God's hands and His will, will be done. I went on to think everything was fine because we were all still smiling and rejoicing regarding my dad's successful heart transplant.

Well, the next morning was a total surprise of chaos, confusion, and humility. My mom and I had planned to go to the hospital. I got up out the bed to get ready and she immediately confronted me about my response from the day before. She explained that she did not like it and it was not nice. I remember explaining to her why I said what I had said and that quieted the controversy for that moment. However, when we got in the car, she began again, expressing how she felt about my seeming disregard for her. I was so confused and wanted it to all just stop.

When confrontation comes, I am a total 'flight' person. I just want to get away from it and dismiss myself from any form of drama. We were driving so I could not flee. At that moment, all kinds of reckless thoughts flooded my mind, but the Holy Spirit quieted them down by telling me to apologize. When my mom finally took a breath, I did just that.

"Momma, all I can do is apologize. I am sorry for what I said and that it hurt you, that was not my intent." I took a breath.

She *said* okay but then went right back into a rant. I could not believe it! I thought the apology was going to extinguish the wildfire, but now it seemed to flare even more. I remember grinding my teeth and holding back the tears as the reckless thoughts started to come back, but again the Holy Spirit said *it is okay, just apologize.* I did again along with expressing that I came back to be there for Daddy and our family in support and love.

These words quenched the flames, and we were able to refocus on my dad's recovery. Even though this was the case, the confusion and suppressed lamenting emotions were still bubbling inside of me. I could not wait to flee, to get back to Arizona, and go straight to the mountain park from the airport to release all of it. When it was time to leave, we were all in a content state giving hugs and kisses as I prepared to return home.

As soon as I got off the plane, I had a one-track mind to get to the mountain park, my own place of worship and release. I yelled, screamed, cried, prayed, and humbled myself before God. I cried out to the Lord about it all. I repented for causing the confusion and for unintentionally hurting my mom. I told him I just did not understand why this has been our relationship for so many years. I prayed over myself and my mom for our relationship to get better.

This was not the first 'bumping of heads' nor the last. But from that point in 2014, things seemed to get better in that the clashes between me and my mom became minimal to none. I would humble myself anytime there was an issue, and regardless if I was at fault or not I would apologize. I would take on the burden of being responsible and walk in humility to resolve the issue. Little did I know, that was like putting a band-aid on a deep cut that needed stitches.

All were mild and seemed to be good until the summer of 2020. One afternoon after work, I called my mom to see how she was doing. We started off having a fun, enjoyable conversation with laughter until I crossed an invisible boundary. I had offended her by reminding her of the teachings she taught me in dealing with a situation she had shared. At that moment, the spirit of offense had taken over. My mom let me know that she felt as though I was attacking her, and I did not need to tell her those things because she knew them, she taught them to me and my sister.

I was completely blown away that this was happening. So, I got offensive that she would even feel attacked by me simply expressing wisdom from her own teachings. Holding back the tears I said, "Momma, I am so sorry. I was not trying to attack you but remind you of what you taught us. I do not know what this thing is that comes between us and causes us to bump heads, but I am going to pray about it because I just do not understand."

The discussion went on until the call ended peacefully. But this is when the war began. I was utterly distraught. After years of peaceful interactions, this bomb just exploded.

Here is my heart stance: for years I had yearned for a normal relationship with my mom. The mother and daughter relationship where we could have open communication, no judgment or criticism, but a genuine connection at least during my adulthood. I prayed over the years asking God to help me be a better daughter and help me with taming my tongue...being quick to listen, slow to speak, and slow to get angry (James 1:19, TPT). I wanted to do the right thing by Him and my mom (James 1:20, TPT). But there was still something unidentifiable about our situation. This last conflict was it for me.

That same evening before I went to bed, I began to war in prayer asking the Lord to reveal to me my issues regarding my mom and how I contribute to the problem. The upcoming year I would celebrate my 40th birthday and I would not go into it with our relationship at odds. Change needed to happen now. I prayed for healing and breakthrough, crying day and night just laying it all at God's feet.

Have you ever wanted something so bad you would do whatever you needed to do to get it? Well, I was determined to have the long-expected relationship with my mom that I knew we were supposed to have. I did not know how to communicate with my mom from that point on because I was too afraid that I would say the wrong thing and cause offense. So, I kept conversations short. I humbled myself before the Lord. I persistently prayed, asking God for the root of this thing between us to be revealed, severed, and consumed by His fire to exist no more.

I did this for a few months declaring peace, healing, revelation, forgiveness, and restoration over our relationship and our entire family. I prayed hard, affirming that the enemy could not have my family, and proclaimed that we belong to Jesus individually, but also as a unit. That we have a ministry together that will be established and thrive for the Kingdom of God.

In time, the Holy Spirit began to reveal things to me. A root of my suppressed memories as a teenager. Some insight into my mom's childhood was identified as another root. It was just enough to understand that the thing between us was beyond us. So, I prayed about them.

In May 2021, I went back to Chicago for a visit to pray with my family and to share a truth with my mom that was revealed from prayer. I did not want to share it, but the Holy Spirit made it clear that I needed to be humble and share it for complete healing.

After sharing, there was more confusion rather than restoration. I did not understand. When I returned to Arizona, I prayed, asking Jesus, what do I do now? I felt as though I had left things with my mom incomplete even though I walked in humility. The Spirit of Counsel advised me to write a letter. I was hesitant to do so at first thinking that my mom would not read it. So I prayed, asking the Holy Spirit to give me the words that I needed to write. I prayed over the letter before, during, and after writing.

Some of the letter read...

"With the Holy Spirits' revelation, I have learned much about the root, which is the enemy. 1. His lies to me and deception as a teenager and young adult, as well as his desire to destroy me, you, my sister, and Daddy...our family. 2. Your childhood... 3. The brittle foundation of Jesus for us both specifically during those times. 4. Spiritual warfare. There are more, but these are the top four.

The past few months of receiving these revelations, it has helped me to have some understanding, healing, and peace. The Lord has helped me to see that it was never you or me all this time, but the enemy behind the scenes. He took advantage of both you and me. Manipulated and exploited our fears, weaknesses, and childhood hurts. All of which we may or may not know existed, but they do. For myself, I had to realize that there was an issue to know to pray to God for revelation, deliverance, healing, and restoration, which is a work in progress now for me. Because I have learned that the real issue is the adversary and his agenda to steal, kill, and destroy our family, I chose to allow the Lord to work on me, my heart, and my mind. It is the only way to achieve the peace I need to move forward in all that He has called me to do.

Now that the adversary has been exposed, it is time for us to do differently and go against what he has stirred up and allow Jesus to repair any damages, heal all wounds, and restore what has been lost. This is the time if you are willing. Willing to let Him renew you, your mind, and your spirit. I am with you as I have started my journey in sowing truth, love, and patience to reap the beautiful relationship we are entitled to, designed by God. God has shown me that it can be so if you are willing.

I love you Momma and I hope that you can forgive me for any hurts that I have unintentionally caused you or done to you. I have asked our Father to forgive me, and I have forgiven myself."

I learned later that this was part of the process of spiritual breakthrough because this letter did not bring restoration. It would not come until five months later when I had to return to Chicago for my grandmother's homegoing celebration. Prior to the visit I had prayed asking the Lord for an opportunity to make amends with my mom during the visit. During my covenant time with Him, He had given me a vision.

In the dining room of my parent's house, one of the chairs from the dining table was facing outward where my mother would sit. There were colorful flowers around the chair in the shape of a horseshoe. I was to kneel in the center of the flowers physically humbling myself before my mom and He gave me words to say. At the end of my covenant time, I simply said, *sure I can do that.*

By the time I made it to Chicago, I had forgotten all about the vision. A day after the service, boom! My mom and I bumped heads, which I would say were our worst ever. Right after the incident, the Holy Spirit brought the vision back to my remembrance, which then made sense.

Hesitant, I asked God, *what if she rejects me? What I am supposed to do?*

He said, *Just do what I showed you and I will take care of the rest.*

So I got the flowers and began to do what I saw in the vision. I led my mom to the chair, and she sat down. I knelt before her, took her hands, and held them. I looked up at her and she looked down at me as tears fell down our faces. I then spoke the words given to me during the time of receiving the vision.

"Momma, I kneel down before you not to worship you, not to praise you, but to honor you as my mother and this is the last act of humility that I have to offer."

The Holy Spirit guided the rest of my words of affirmation and love to her (Exodus 20:12, NKJV). After ten minutes or so, I was able to get up. I told her I loved her and in so many words let her know that the adversary cannot win. We hugged, kissed, dried each other's tears, and rejoiced. The breakthrough happened at that moment!

From that point on, I have been praising and worshipping God with thanksgiving for the amazing changes that had immediately taken place. This one act of humility resulted in a *1 Peter 5:6*, turnaround! He blessed us both with the beautiful relationship we desired.

I think about where my mom and I are today with our renewed relationship. It is not perfect. It is a work in progress. But it is better than it has ever been! I have been thinking about this and realized that had I chosen at any point during this process to be prideful. If I believed that I did not need to be the one to pray and humble myself. If I pointed the finger at my mom and questioned, *what about her*? The rewards of a renewed relationship, breakthrough, forgiveness, healing, and joy would not have manifested.

One of the lessons learned from this is that if I humble myself before ABBA Father, walking in humility is that much easier. Also, *Humility* is living like Jesus Christ. He is the King of Kings and Lord of Lords. Yet, He humbled Himself in many different ways while here on Earth, doing the Father's will by serving others. In John 13:3-5 (MSG), He washed His disciple's feet. Then He said to do as He did...be humble and serve others to receive the reward of experiencing a life of happiness enriched with untold blessings.[11]

As I practice walking in humility daily, life gets better and better. I am experiencing the promise of God's happiness enriched with untold blessings. I am still a work in progress trying to live as Jesus did. He is my idol and His perfect example of how to do the will of the Father, reminds me to be humble as a requirement to please God.[12]

Chapter 5

Building in Belief

by Shyla Bassey

When Doubt Gets in the Way

Have you ever doubted yourself? Doubted your ability? Doubted your strength? Doubted your decisions? How did you overcome that doubt?

These questions represent a constant tug of war many of us face between fear/doubt & belief/faith. You have probably seen the acronym, F.E.A.R (False Evidence Appearing Real). Although I believe this concept to be true, life creates experiences that can alter our belief system to make the false evidence appear to be very *Real* and quite intimidating.

Biblically, we see this in Mark's Gospel, chapter nine, when the father with the possessed son tells Jesus, "I do believe; help me overcome my unbelief!" It's an honest reflection of how, in our humanity, we struggle with the *false evidence appearing real* in our lives even while we desire to believe God for *greater*. The fact was that the father's son was indeed severely ill, afflicted, and demon-possessed. The father said his son had been that way since he was a child, so we can assume a long time.

The desperate father tried getting Jesus' disciples to help and they could not. We could also assume that he had already sought the help of many other professionals and religious leaders over the years with no result. So understandably, the man was left disillusioned and his faith severely shaken which lead to F.E.A.R that a change would never come. But, we know he had not given up all hope (faith) because he was still seeking help.

Yet, the father was very doubtful when *Help* showed up. Could this Teacher actually succeed where everyone else had failed? Jesus perceived the father's fearful doubts and called *it* out, giving the father a chance to be vulnerable about his own heart posture. After the man gave an honest confession, we see Jesus' heart response is to help the father's *unbelief*. Jesus heals the boy! This is God's faith-building in action.

Cultivating a belief mindset

Belief has been something that needed cultivating in my own life. In 2018, I began the process of obtaining my Series 7 – Registered Representative License, which involved taking a six-hour long, two-hundred-and-fifty-question exam. Challenging myself has always been the standard and this was the Mt. Everest of all goals I had aimed to achieve. The preparation for this exam required a strenuous seven-week self-study plan with over 300+ Hours of study time. Passing the exam meant more doors opened, giving me access to advance my career at my current financial institution, and in the banking and brokerage industry as a whole.

The stakes were high. And doubt began to settle in as soon as the study materials arrived. Imagine receiving three encyclopedias and being told everything is important and is testable! My immediate reaction was, *What did I sign myself up for?* and *How am I gonna be able to do this?* Which would later turn into, *I've got this!* This sequence occurred throughout my entire study period.

It was a constant wavering in my beliefs, emotional roller coaster, and stinking thinking. Many trending positivity ideologies will have you believe that getting rid of negative thinking altogether yields success. "ALWAYS think positive," is the running slogan. However, they don't tell you that stinking thinking and doubting yourself is something you have to process through by pressing forward even while you're scared. And admitting you're scared is sometimes the first step toward your positive outcome. Remember that weary dad seeking Jesus' help?

Processing through is submitting your resume to the company even while you struggle with the belief that you're unqualified for the job. Showing up to the gym every day, even while you're depressed about your current health status and it seems impossible to change. If you were to wait for your feelings to turn positive and beliefs to align before you take action, you may find yourself stuck indefinitely. Don't let the wavering beliefs discourage you or keep you in a sunken depressed state. It is a real part of the process. But know that God has you covered.

What I know to be certain is that when God opens a door, He definitely wants us to make it through it. He is building your faith even while he is processing you out of doubt, and ushering you through the open door of your *greater*! Overcoming that doubt, however, can be an impossible feat without belief. The father with the demon-possessed son still had belief (or hope/faith) even while he doubted. The critical mindset shift to become dedicated and determined to believe that what you desire is possible requires repetition.

Repetition means showing up every day, and building consistency while you're faithing your way through a difficult journey. Repetition means repeating God's word and affirmations to yourself when those negative thoughts rumble under the surface, thwarting those fiery darts aimed at your heart. Repetition means dusting yourself off, and getting back into position when stinking thinking bubbles up, penetrating the surface and knocking you off course. Repetition means to keep going and keep believing no matter what circumstance presents itself causing you to shake in your faith. This is how you cultivate (develop) your faith.

Faith without works is dead

We can say we believe but do nothing to prepare for what we're believing God for. Our preparation efforts actually show we are faithing-it (faith in action). We are believing God by putting in work. Succumbing to nonbelief actually leads to procrastination and a "why even try" attitude.

I believe this is why in chapter two of James' Epistle, he explains why faith without action is dead. If a person wanted to improve their overall health, and believed it could change, should they just lay in bed all day eating junkfood, watching television, waiting for the changes they want to see appear? Or will they need to make an effort to adjust their diet and physical activity? This may mean seeking support as well. Like James, they are demonstrating their faith by their action.

Nine hour days, six to seven days out of the week, enclosed in my apartment's business center, I was burrowed in books. I canceled all distractions from noise to phone calls and even deleted my social media apps. From sunrise to sunset I studied and did what I needed to do to properly prepare myself.

I knew what to expect at the end of my study sessions—a quiz or an exam. In order to progress and remain on target, a passing quiz was necessary for each end-of-chapter review. Reading and comprehending the information felt simple in the beginning until I hit a roadblock, my first exam.

That first exam was an overview of all concepts in the first six chapters of the book. These were timed to train you in how to pace yourself while test taking. Things were moving smoothly through the exam until I reached the halfway point an hour and a half later. I began to feel overwhelmed as the questions became more challenging, the process of elimination shifted to guessing, and I began questioning the countless hours I had studied before taking the exam. As the clock was racing, I had to keep going and answer to the best of my knowledge. And my anxiety levels were throwing me off my game. Finally, the timer went off and my final score was provided. I scored sixty-five percent. Seventy-two was needed. I was several percentage points away from being able to proceed to the next section.

It was a dagger plunged deep. I reminded myself that although shaken, I was not destroyed. I regrouped and pressed on. You see, circumstances will arise, presenting themselves as *real*, and trying to convince you that all the effort you've made has been for nothing. *Why not give up and stop while you're ahead?* But you must double back to the truth that God did not bring you up to this point to leave you. And when you refocus your stance and adjust your faith-goggles, you'll see God in the midst of the cloud of doubt.

God solidifies your belief

God showed me signs throughout this journey that enabled me to shift my focus from doubt to faith. Several weeks into studying, the feeling of overwhelm took over. I searched for resources high and low and identified a supplemental book to support my studies. One day, as I was wrapping up my studies for the evening, a bookmark fell out of the used book that I had purchased and it read, *"GOD HAS A PURPOSE FOR YOUR LIFE!"*

I released the deepest sigh and was engulfed with emotions as I saw this profound confirmation. Reading this bookmark became a daily task to set my mind at ease. Understanding the power that our internal thoughts become external manifestations, I drenched myself in affirmations such as, "I Am intelligent!", "I Am a conqueror!", "I Am an achiever!", "I am walking in my purpose!" All of these "I Am" affirmations became part of my daily self-talk.

Faith is something that is not physically tangible, it is a strong belief in an idea. In the letter to the Hebrews, the Apostle Paul defines faith as "the substance of things hoped for, the evidence of things not seen." In English grammar, faith is an abstract noun, meaning like love it is nonphysical, an idea that can only be seen by evidence of its manifestation. For me, faith was believing I would pass this test not because I had done it before, not because I had physical proof that I could, but based on the work I put in and God affirming my efforts.

Reflecting and repeating affirmations began to shift my perspective from focusing solely on the outcome to trusting the process. This elevated my confidence in my ability to execute and move forward courageously. Navigating through a new challenge, I had to remember that our thoughts become behaviors and every positive word mattered to support increasing my internal self-talk.

Three days before the big exam, I had a scheduled call to review any topics with an instructor. The intention of this call was to discuss challenging questions and any final test-taking skills that needed refreshing. Our conversation quickly transitioned from exam prep to her asking me, "*Shyla, do you believe in John 3:16?*"

Stunningly, I responded, "Absolutely!"

She proceeded to ask, "*Did you recently get baptized in the last year or so?*"

I was completely astonished! You see, I had taken the step to be re-baptized at the beginning of that year.

She then shared, "*I'm not sure why, but God wants me to tell you that, He is pleased, continue to shine your light so that others can see!*"

We spent nearly an hour sharing our spiritual journeys and the power of this unexpected, yet needed conversation. The message was very clear–**faith will always beat fear.**

God kept affirming me and it solidified my faith in the greatest possible way! He made me secure in Him and renewed my value in myself. What it taught me was no matter the uphill battles I had to endure, *greater* was on the other side, and that I was built for it. It taught me to embrace the process, by truly living and breathing in each moment. I saw God in new and real ways that strengthened me and further matured me as a Believer to show up whole even in other parts of my life. Find grace in your growing pains by releasing yourself to God as humble clay in the hands of the potter.

The big test day had arrived. While my nerves were still high, I walked in with a sense of calm. After completing the first half of the exam, my immediate emotion resorted back to doubt as I did not feel confident in some of the responses. However, I knew there would still be a chance with the second half of the exam. I headed over to the cafe to refuel and prepare for the next three hours. I ordered a simple breakfast meal and God sent me another reminder to keep my faith high. My order totaled $7.77. The biblical number of completion! This immediately energized my spirit and I was able to walk back with complete confidence and full faith that I would pass.

Six hours later, I passed!

This Journey taught me the importance of ensuring that our faith becomes greater than our fears. Always remember that God is always there. He will never put more on us than we can bear because He actually bears the burden of it all if we allow Him. He answers our prayers. It's on us to recognize, identify and accept the answer He gives us.

God is building your belief as you build *it*. No matter what the task, trip, job, or experience that you are pursuing, no matter what you are building, hold this scripture in your heart:

> *"Trust in the LORD with all of your heart and lean not on your own understanding. In all your ways submit to Him, and He will make your paths straight."*[13]

Chapter 6

Building in Influence

by Robin K. Butler

Influence: *The capacity to have an effect on the character, development, or behavior of someone or something, or the effect itself.* [14]

What are you working on? What are your desires, dreams, and goals? When you think of the light at the end of the tunnel, what does the journey look like getting there? Who or what has influenced you? All interesting points to ponder.

If you sit and think for a moment, I guarantee you'll realize that the power of influence has shown up in your life repeatedly. We've grown from the little boy or girl who experienced peer pressure and was negatively impacted; into the man or woman who is connecting with peers and impacting lives positively. Influence, my friends, is powerful and priceless!

Like many, I've done quite a bit of reflection over the years and have continued to lean into my **purpose**, **passion**, and **potential** (three keys we will use as our anchor to navigate influence building). I've been sharing messages with similar themes as a speaker, coach, and educator for quite some time with my family, friends, and colleagues. They all know somewhere in our discussion, Robin is going to talk about the significance of influence. They may tease me about it, but I know they are listening.

When we think of building ourselves while we build others, we must realize that influence is an 'inside' job. I coined a phrase that there must be *Inward reflection, for Outward reward*. So first things first, we must be partakers of what it means to have influence in our lives before we can truly influence others. Interestingly this makes me think of the safety message we hear when we travel by airplane, "put on your mask first!" How can we save (influence) others, when we don't have the oxygen for ourselves?

I found myself leaning into the work of Dr. John C. Maxwell, Dr. Maya Angelou, Dr. Robert Cialdini, Dr. Myles Monroe, Dr. Dennis Kimbro, Bishop T.D. Jakes, Napoleon Hill, Bonnie St. John, Brene' Brown, Simon Sinek, Daniel Goleman, and countless thought leaders when I reflect on my journey of influence. Who you listen to and follow really matters when you desire influence in your life. We want to be associated with something or someone. We live in a social media age of like, subscribe, or follow. It is important that we connect with and to the right influencers for our next level of growth.

I desire to have more influence and leave this world empty. For me, that would mean I didn't waste God's time with my purpose and the potential he put inside of me. I often share what I call invaluable leadership lessons because my mission is to be a person of value by being intentional, influential, and impactful. One of my invaluable leadership lessons is about influence.

I believe a person can shift the climate of a room or the trajectory of an experience by using their influence. This starts with their intention, and as a result, there is an impact. You may disagree, but I would argue that influence is more valuable than money. It's been said that money can buy anything; but I would debate this philosophy, money cannot buy influence. If you think about it like this it's access versus excess. The excess gives you access, so excess may be the resources you possess and it is the excess that leads to the access. Some things are well beyond our efforts, therefore access leads to influence. You can have the resources, money, talent, and gifts, but if you don't have access how will anyone know about your brilliance or influence?

If we truly want to build ourselves, while we build others, our goal should be to erase the finish line and to keep going. We never know what we might achieve or how we could influence others if we come to an abrupt halt in our journey to influence. Influence is one of those character traits that is like a muscle. The more you work it, the better it becomes. I can remember working out with my personal trainer at six am in the morning. I didn't love getting up, nor the routine of exercise, but I loved the results. I would jokingly tell him that we had a love-hate relationship. I loved the results but hated the work. However, it was a part of the process. It was his influence and experience coupled with my intention that yielded the impactful outcome for me.

What happens when we desire to increase our influence? I think it starts with being intentional. We consider our daily practices and routines. What are you doing at six am, ten am, or nine pm? Influential people have a rhythm and routine to their day. Are you setting an intention for your day? What is your plan? Your intention should flow right into your level of influence because influence doesn't just happen, we must do something actionable. After you've done some reflection and put some habits into practice, ultimately your influence becomes impactful.

How we use our influence is important. We all have it in some form or fashion at different levels. My desire to influence comes from the many leaders and influencers in my life. I want to be a catalyst and create a spark to L.E.A.D. This acronym means I want to influence others to *learn, enrich, aspire,* and *discover* their **purpose**, **passion**, and **potential**. When we learn about influence, we can enrich the lives of others and aspire to help them become more impactful because we have discovered our purpose, passion, and potential. I believe that this directly ties to our influence. In essence, you can't really influence when you don't have the experience.

When I think of where I am and where I am going, the following words resonate with me, intentional, influential, and impactful. I believe that in order to do and be more, we must fully embrace our ability to be influencers and our influence. This can't be accomplished without truly understanding our **purpose, passion,** and **potential**.

When someone *conceives an idea*, it is in their 'head' where the concept begins, which leads to the discovery of **purpose**. When one *believes*, it is in their 'heart', often we are moved to do something and we block out fear, pain, or other emotions, which results in a strong **passion** for or against something. Our belief system is tied to our hearts. Lastly, when we *achieve*, it is about an accomplishment of a goal that encompasses all of our future plans, visions, hopes, and dreams for what we desire in life. Growth nor goals can be achieved without doing something. So growth and goals are tied to our 'hands', which uncover and tap into our **potential**. There is so much fulfillment in knowing who you are as well as who you are not. When we understand who we are and how we are designed to influence others, we can live a fulfilled life. Living an influential life causes one to yield to transformation or as I prefer to say, "a metamorphosis." As we lean into influence we move from mundane to magnificent or as I've coined *sufficient to significant*.

Thought leader, Robert B. Cialdini, Ph.D. once said, "It is through the influence process that we generate and manage change." In his studies, he outlined six universal principles of influence, which are useful and effective in a wide range of circumstances. The essential principles are reciprocity, scarcity, authority, commitment and consistency, liking, and consensus (or social proof).

When we think of reciprocity, we often put this into practice. People are willing to do something for you if you've done something nice or advantageous for them.

Let's consider scarcity, we influence with scarcity often in sales settings. Think about how many times, you were thinking it was the 'last one' or a particular offer would no longer be available.

Often authority deals with knowledge and the ability to influence because of that awareness. If people believe you are a subject matter expert, then your expertise is less likely to be challenged. People who are perceived as authoritative, credible, and experts in their fields are more influential and persuasive than those who are not. This has a lot to do with the core of trust.

We are more likely to follow someone when we trust them. Inconsistency and lack of commitment are two ways to quickly ruin your reputation. Consistency and commitment are vital. People must see you being committed and consistent before they commit to your vision. In essence, you must model consistency before gaining buy-in. Once you provide the blueprint, then they will feel more compelled to agree and do the same.

The likeability factor is important in influence. It may be totally obvious, but people are often influenced by those individuals that they like versus those they don't. There are many benefits to diversity; however, human nature often causes us to migrate toward those who are similar to us. Humans are social by nature and want to feel a sense of belonging. As independent as we like to portray ourselves, many of us would rather be a part of something or a group. We like the suggestions of others and we often look around us to see what others are doing before we make a decision. We may not verbalize it, but we all want to be accepted and not ostracized.

3P Soup and Influence

I've arrived at the place in life where my desire is to inspire intention that sparks influence and impact to intersect with purpose and passion that culminates with exceeded potential.

I learned some time ago that "Leadership is influence, nothing more nothing less," according to leadership guru, John C. Maxwell.

When I was a little girl, I can recall my mother making various meals, sometimes there was a routine and on certain days, we knew what we were going to eat for dinner. Often Wednesday was spaghetti day and it lasted two days. Friday was fish day, and one of the very few days we got fried food. We're from Louisiana, so southern cooking and hospitality were a part of my mother's daily routine. She was very adamant about us eating dinner together. On the weekends, my father prepared breakfast. His pancake recipe is still in rotation and is now a grand and great-grand favorite. At every meal, we would say our grace and be thankful for what we had. Isn't influence interesting? I have four siblings and now that I reflect on it, my parents influenced us and many of these traditions we have carried into our own families.

When it got cold, my mother would make soup. I wasn't really a soup fan, but back then, we ate what was put in front of us. My mother would make the infamous gumbo, which we all loved as a New Orleans tradition. She would also make chicken noodle soup. I wasn't a fan of peas, so I'd pick them out. Some days she'd prepare meals with mashed potatoes and peas as the sides and I despised those days because I thought peas were just green and yucky. I clearly can hear her saying, "they may not be good to you right now, but they are good for you." My mother really knew how to influence the outcome.

It's taken some time, but I now eat peas and realize their benefits as a vegetable. As I got older, I started to write about *3P* Soup, in a figurative sense. Add **Purpose**, **Passion**, and **Potential**, mix it with some other ingredients that lead to Intention, Influence, and Impact, and you have a gourmet meal!

Just as with my parents, I was influenced by former leaders and the impact that many of them had on me was life-changing. It's been said that people come into our lives for reasons or seasons. I'm grateful for the reasons and seasons of those who have influenced me from my parents to pastors, managers, coaches, mentors, and the like. It has shaped me into who I am today.

There are some things to remember as we explore and connect the dots to further understand the role of influence and how we must build our own influence while helping others to build their influence. Remember you are not alone in this process of building. Influence is like a muscle. Strength training it is something that we must do regularly to become more effective.

Purpose: Calling and Competence to Influence

As we reflect on purpose, it is tied to our calling and our competence to influence. Who is your audience, and who do you desire to impact? Do you have the knowledge and skill to do so? These are questions we begin with when we assess where we are and where we want to be or go. So often people have the confidence to influence but lack the call or competence and it can be disastrous. Before we can lead others, we must be able to lead and influence ourselves.

Passion: Character and Connection to Influence

It is vital to know who we are and who we are not. Our character goes before us and often speaks loudly before we ever open our mouths. Let's think about a stage play, characters serve as the driving force to bring the story to life. If this is the case in a stage play, what role are you playing when it comes to your character and influence? Be passionate about your character and connecting to others to influence them to their highest good. It's been said that sometimes, you may be the only 'bible' people read. What would the book say about your character and ability to lead with influence? Maya Angelou is frequently cited, "People will forget what you said, people will forget what you did, but people will never forget how you made them feel." Influence is the ability to lead with our heart to connect and engage to foster an experience.

There is no doubt that taking the one step of connecting with more people will improve your influence. This means more than just having someone sign up for your newsletter or follow you on various social platforms. It means going the extra mile and reaching out to people, helping them using any means possible, and sometimes just having a conversation.

It is such a simple concept, yet one that eludes many. Too often, the focus of connection is to try and sell or determine what's in it for me. This should be the last possible motivation when making your connections. There is nothing wrong with trying to make some money using your connections, but let's just learn to connect authentically. Look at it this way, the operative word when connecting with others is give. Always be willing to give way more than you take. Become a resource, learn about what people are looking for, and give it to them. I look at it like this, *connection is the new currency*, when it comes to influence. It should flow just like money.

Potential: Commitment and Capacity to Influence

We have heard that our perception is typically our reality. What people see is critical to how they perceive your commitment and capacity to influence. We don't like to hear it, but consistency is key. Consistency comes into play once again and we must strive to be present, honest, caring, and dedicated to inspiring others. To inspire loyalty, you must have a track record of what I coined as leading with H.E.A.R.T. (honesty, equity, accountability, resiliency, and transparency).

People desire to be heard, they want to know you value them and are listening to them. This is a major part of our commitment and capacity to influence. Simply taking the time to listen to others makes them feel valued, even if you don't accept their ideas. If a follower or employee perhaps feels ignored and there's no point talking to you, they won't. They will soon disengage from your vision and ultimately follow you and your instructions begrudgingly.

If you are viewed as the leader (influencer) who goes above and beyond, your team is more likely to go the extra mile for you and your clients. If you avoid people and you aren't visible, you may be perceived as disinterested, unprepared, uninformed, and lacking the credibility to lead. Many successful leaders make it a point to be visible and engaged with their followers. Our potential is actionable and we should be found serving others and making a difference.

So again, my friend, do you desire to influence? First understand your **purpose**, **passion**, and **potential** which helps you to build *You*. From there you can build others because you've put into practice being intentional, influential, and impactful. Take the leap to understand your <u>calling and competence</u> to influence, your <u>character and connection</u> to influence, and your <u>commitment and capacity</u> to influence. You'll be well on your way in your journey to influence.

As an influencer, you're not conceiving, believing, and achieving simply for your own happiness. Even so, we must first embrace influence for ourselves before we build others. People need what you have to offer and the world is waiting on you. Think about it this way, a gift is never meant to sit under a tree or in a dark closet unopened, right? In order for it to be classified as a gift, it must be given to someone. Our gifts and talents are meant to be shared, so we can connect, collaborate, and celebrate. We are indeed blessed to be a blessing to others. Go out, make a difference, and add value by using your influence to build your family, career, ministry, and/or business.

Chapter 7

Building in Expansion

by Tiffany Hodgest

Help, I'm being expanded!

Expand: *to increase the extent, volume, or scope of; enlarge.*[1]

Expansion: *the act or process of expanding; the quality or state of being expanded.*[2]

One evening during my time of worship and prayer, the Spirit of the Lord dropped this passage of scripture.

Isaiah 54:2-4 (ESV, emphasis added):

"Enlarge the place of your tent, and let the curtains of your habitations be stretched out; spare not; lengthen your cords and strengthen your stakes,

For you will spread abroad to the right hand and to the left, and your offspring will possess the nations and make the desolate cities to be inhabited.

Fear not, for you shall not be ashamed; neither be confounded nor depressed, for you shall not be put to shame. For you shall forget the shame of your youth and you shall not remember the reproach of your widowhood anymore."

I knew immediately why. The Lord was telling me to prepare to be *stretched*. The Lord was preparing me for more! It was time to increase my capacity to *do* more and *receive* more from God. I also sensed that the Lord was broadening my sphere of influence in this season of my life. A few days later, the Holy Spirit told me it was time to write my book. Not long after that, I was presented with the opportunity. I *knew* this was God! I was grateful for the opportunity but fear made me question myself and my ability to write. I began to question if my voice could be heard among so many other excellent writers.

It was at that point I recognized my mindset had to be challenged! I had to break out of this way of thinking or I would forever run from things that pushed me and stretched me, *built* me for greater. That is when I understood that my *expansion* and the ability to increase my capacity were dependent upon my perspective. If I continued to think small then I would continue to *do* little and *possess* little. God was requiring more *of* me and more *from* me.

In Isaiah 54:3, the Prophet proclaims, "For you will spread abroad to the right hand and to the left, and your offspring will possess the nations and make the desolate cities to be inhabited." After reading this, the Holy Spirit revealed to me, *You can't possess nations with a mediocre mindset!* I could no longer allow my past, insecurities, fear, and comparison to others, keep me from obeying God.

The phrases, **"spare not"** and **"strengthen your stakes"** in verse two of Isaiah 54 (ESV) stood out to me.

"Enlarge the place of your tent, and let the curtains of your habitations be stretched out; ***spare not****; lengthen your cords and* ***strengthen your stakes.****"*

These two words in this verse brought me to a *Selah* moment, causing me to pause and think. What was the Lord saying to me? Why did these words stir me in such a way?

I could no longer spare myself the stretching and forgo this place of enlargement. I could no longer shrink back in fear, and be comfortable where I was. In fact, I had to reject small thinking altogether. I had to reject the box in which I had allowed myself and others to keep me. When I began to think about the words **"strengthen your stakes,"** I knew this enlargement would cause me to dig deeper. Not only would I have to dig deeper within myself, but this would require a deeper relationship with the Lord.

> **"As for everyone who comes to me and hears my words and puts them into practice, I will show you what they are like. They are like a man building a house, who dug down deep and laid the foundation on the rock. When a flood came, the torrent struck that house but could not shake it, because it was well built"** (Luke 6:47-48, NIV).

This scripture reminds me of how skyscrapers are built. When building these massive structures, the builders have to dig deep into the ground to find soil sturdy enough to hold the weight of the building. This also prevents the winds and other natural forces from toppling it over. In other words, my foundation in the Lord for this season has to be stronger. I had to strengthen my stakes in God to ensure that what He was building within me did not fall. I needed to be sure that when outside forces and winds came I could continue to stand and build.

The Demand To Expand

In order to have a demand for expansion, the maximum capacity must first be reached. For example, any business is able to operate when its maximum capacity has been reached. However, the business will never be able to serve more than their posted occupancy if they never expand. This failure hinders that business from reaching its full potential. It is the same with us, we are still able to operate if we avoid the demand to expand, but we fail to realize the greatness and the ability to do more if we *refuse* to expand. Understand that God will never ask you to do something that you don't have the ability to do. So, if He is asking you to increase your capacity, then you have to recognize that He sees more inside you than you see in yourself.

Genesis 13:14-17

> "The Lord said to Abram after Lot had parted from him, "Look around from where you are, to the north and south, to the east and west. All the land that you see I will give to you and your offspring forever. I will make your offspring like the dust of the earth, so that if anyone could count the dust, then your offspring could be counted. Go, walk through the length and breadth of the land, for I am giving it to you." (NIV)

Abram was already a wealthy man when God told him to look to the north and south, to the east and west. God told Abram, **"as far as your eyes can see is yours, I will make your offspring like the dust of the earth."** When God said this to Abram he had not yet fathered any children. This was a *demand* to *expand* for Abram. Abram and his family had outgrown the land, yet God was giving Abram more. The Lord was preparing Abram to possess nations.

If Abram was to become *Abraham*, the Father of Many Nations, he had to adjust his mind to what the Lord was showing him, he could no longer be satisfied in his current place. He could no longer be satisfied with his current success and wealth. He had to trust God, that he had the capacity within himself to fill the land. He had to *believe* that he was the Father of Many Nations, and *believe* that God was expanding his sphere of influence.

There is a demand to expand upon us as well. Like Abram, we have to trust God and adjust to what He is showing us. You have a Father in Heaven who knows the greatness that is in you. You may have accomplished much, but God wants to give you more. Set your eyes on what He has given you and go possess the Land! Walk boldly into this new place of authority and influence.

With Honor Comes Expansion

1 Chronicles 4:9-10

> "Jabez was more honorable than his brothers. His mother had named him Jabez, saying, "I gave birth to him in pain." Jabez cried out to the God of Israel, "Oh, that you would bless me and enlarge my territory! Let your hand be with me, and keep me from harm so that I will be free from pain." And God granted his request." (NIV)

Verse 9 of 1 Chronicles 4 reveals that Jabez was more honorable than his brothers. Jabez was given his name because his mother gave birth to him in pain. Yet still, Jabez was a righteous man. In other words, regardless of your past, live a life of honor. God is not going to enlarge your place of influence if you are not living an honorable life. Do we honor and obey God first and foremost? Do we honor the things of God? Do we honor the kingdom relationships that God has given us?

The purpose of your enlargement and your expansion is for God to get the glory out of your life. You are the vessel God has chosen and you should not take the Glory. I believe Jabez was a man that understood this. Jabez's prayer in verse 10: **"Jabez cried out to the God of Israel, 'Oh, that you would bless me and enlarge my territory! Let your hand be with me, and keep me from harm so that I will be free from pain.' And God granted his request."** Jabez asked God to bless him and enlarge his territory, but he also asked God's Hand to be with him and keep him from harm. Jabez knew the importance of the Hand of the Lord being with him, and knew it wouldn't be a true blessing without it.

We can't build, enlarge, or expand without the Hand of the Lord being upon us and *with* us. It is God who will cause our lives to prosper and enlarge our territory. It is God who will bless and strengthen us. It is God who will keep us from harm and free us from pain. It is God who will ultimately grant our request

It's In You

In essence, nothing and no one can stop us from building and expanding, because we all have the supernatural ability within us to create, build, and expand. Genesis 1:26a reveals, **"And God said, Let us make man in our image, after our likeness."** Our Heavenly Father created man, built the world, expanded the land and the seas. Read that again! *We were created in His image and His likeness.* Due to this, we can create, we can build and we can expand. It is our failure to renew our minds, change our perspective, increase our capacity, and honor God that prevents us from expanding.

I decree that these failures can no longer prevent you from walking in your potential. I declare that you are now moving in the exact timing of the Lord. Upon reading this, may you be provoked to build and expand. It's time to build more! It's time to expand! You have reached your maximum capacity at this level. Prepare for the stretching and understand that there's more inside of you. Believe that you have the supernatural ability to do all that God is requiring of you!

Let Us Pray: *Father, in the name of Jesus I praise you for being an Omniscient God. You know the innermost parts of me. You are the Master Creator and Master Builder, you have the blueprints of my life. I honor you first and foremost. I vow to live a life of honor and righteousness before you.*

I reject small thinking and I come out of agreement with mediocracy. It is you that is bringing me into a place of enlargement. So, I enlarge the place of my tent and let the curtains of my habitations be stretched out. I lengthen my cords and allow the stretching. I accept the demand to expand so that I may reach my full potential in this season. I strengthen my stakes to dig a deep and strong foundation in you.

Father, I trust that You know what you're doing. I release you to pull everything out of me that will produce the greatness that You see. I will not allow fear, comparison, and insecurity to hinder me any longer. God, you get the glory out of my life. Enlarge my territory, increase my capacity, strengthen me, prepare me, build me and grant my request in the Mighty Name of Jesus. Amen.

Chapter 8

Building in Excellence

by Dr. Ansonya L. Pace-Burke

As you strive towards becoming an excellent leader, let this principle: "Building me while I'm Building in Excellence" become your catchphrase.

Remember that God has deposited the seed of greatness and an excellent spirit in you. However, He doesn't stop at that point. He is interested in helping you grow by showing you the tremendous power in you and how you can activate it and use it to impact (*build*) your world better.

At every point of your life, God holds you by your hand, guiding and leading you where you will meet people who will become instrumental in your transformational journey of excellent leadership.

He also leads you to places and experiences that will help refine the raw potential inside of you and make them more valuable. The experiences you face might sometimes be tough and challenging but know that they are not coincidental but divinely orchestrated for your benefit. Therefore, God is building you for excellence. He is preparing you for the big stage and the limelight.

However, understanding you have an excellent spirit and that God is working in you is not the endpoint. You also have the responsibility to build others.

God is building you to empower and prepare you to build others. He has opened your eyes to see that your dreams and goals, no matter how great, can be achieved so you can have the confidence to challenge others to rise and pursue excellence.

Who is an Excellent Leader?

The term excellent leadership is not an attempt to paint a picture of perfection or a leadership style without errors. It is a fact that perfection is not realistic or attainable, and mistakes are the roadway to becoming better and tapping into one's inner power and potential. That being said, excellent leadership refers to the qualities of an authentic leader.

So, what makes one an excellent leader?

An excellent leader works with people.

According to Eleanor Roosevelt, "A good leader inspires people to have confidence in the leader, a great leader inspires people to have confidence in themselves."

To become an excellent leader, you must understand that it's not about you but the people. An excellent leader always takes the backstage and allows the people to be in the spotlight. They don't have to be everywhere and do everything. Instead, they know how to inspire people to get the work done and achieve an objective.

An excellent leader builds leaders.

A weak leader finds satisfaction in people depending on them. Therefore, they always seek to find more and more followers to massage their egos.

However, an excellent leader focuses on building more leaders. Excellent leadership is about letting people understand the magnitude of potential and power they possess and showing them how to utilize their abilities without waiting for instructions before they act.

An excellent leader understands that he is incapable of doing the work alone. So, he empowers people through training, guidance, and mentorship, enabling them to seize the initiative.

An excellent leader leads.

It sounds like a tautology, right? But unfortunately, many so-called leaders do not lead. They hardly do what they say.

An excellent leader must always be at the forefront. He must talk the talk and walk the walk. Anybody can have a dream and set high goals, but only exceptional people put in the necessary work even when it is not convenient to actualize the dream.

An excellent leader does not only inspire by word of mouth; he rolls up his sleeves and gets his hands dirty. People trust you as a leader when you deliver results.

Excellent leaders work on themselves.

You cannot change others unless you have changed yourself. To become an excellent leader, you must start by changing your behaviors, values, belief systems, circle of influence, etc. Only then can you change the people around you. Who you are and who you are becoming determines the kind of leader you will become. Therefore, you must seek self-mastery and personal development consistently to unravel your creative genius and become the best version of yourself.

God is Excellent

A glance in the mirror gives you the perfect vision of who made you. Taking a step further to learn about how your body functions and the beautiful complexity of the human anatomy will unlock your humility and reverence for the excellent designer of the greatest invention ever, God.

Taking a step outside your house and gazing at nature–the beautiful landscape, the vastness of the sea, the grasses and flowers of the fields, all living creatures, great and small, will give you a clear picture of unmatched ingenuity!

However, God's excellence is not limited to creation alone. His entire nature exudes excellence, including leadership.

Although omnipresent and omniscient, we see how God uses mortals to fulfill His desires. He prefers *works* through people to doing things Himself, even though He can achieve anything in a twinkle of an eye. That is what excellent leadership is all about: harnessing people's potential, helping them discover who they are, and achieving outstanding results.

As recorded in the Bible, God uses misfits like David, Moses, etc., to break protocols and achieve monumental successes. He appointed the feeble and fearful like Gideon, making him a mighty warrior who defeated the ferocious Midianites' army. He made a slave boy like Joseph a Prime Minister in a foreign land and made Paul, a former notorious persecutor of Christians, a key personality in propagating the Gospel.

God specializes in qualifying the unqualified and strengthening the weak. He gives visions and dreams, empowering people to achieve them even when such dreams seem impossible. For example, He gave Joseph a dream that he would become a great person people would bow down to and honor. However, his reality and the events that later unfolded in his life didn't match the dream. Joseph's brother sold him into slavery, and at a point, he became a prisoner in Egypt. But God was with him throughout his trying times until he became Prime Minister of the then world power.

An excellent leader never deserts his people but pushes them to go beyond their limitations, shortcomings, and challenges, and this is what God does.

Be Excellent as God is Excellent

God created you in His image (Genesis 1:27). This means you have the seed of excellence buried in your system. In the Bible, you're referred to as a god (Psalm 82:6). You have all it takes to imagine, create, and lead like God.

God has given you tremendous power to do extraordinary things and cause a change in this world (Genesis 1:28). However, you must be willing to nurture that seed of excellence in you by first accepting that *you* can be excellent. It is time to change your mindset to believe that you are built for greatness and nothing short of that. Work and walk with the understanding that you are not just another human being occupying space on earth but a change agent who has the spirit of excellence and incredible power!

The next thing you must do is activate excellence. Be intentional about acting excellently. Distinguish yourself to stand out among the crowd. Don't be afraid to challenge the norm or start new conversations. Let your presence be felt positively when you enter a room, and let your absence be felt when you step out.

Aim for the stars. Don't sell yourself short. Think about big ideas and seek for the resources to achieve them. God spoke the earth into form. Therefore, say only positive things because your tongue has the power to create or destroy.

Excellence in Ministry and Marketplace

Every Christian is called to ministry. Mounting the podium and holding a microphone is not the only evidence of being in ministry. Your ministry involves how you live your life at home, in society, and in your business or place of work.

Every area of your life, including the marketplace, is your place of ministry. It is a platform for you to stand out in your conduct, how you treat people and do your work. Whether you are in full-time ministry or not, God expects you to be excellent in all your dealings.

You need three things to achieve excellence in ministry and the marketplace: **Dedication, Focus, and the Holy Spirit**.

This first requires dedication to excellence in your ministry and the marketplace. It begins with an excellent mindset. Make up your mind not to do anything short of excellence. There are already more than enough good people. The world needs *excellent* people in ministry and the marketplace. Extra effort, diligence, consistency, and discipline will get you there.

Next, you need to focus. In a world where there are so many distractions, being focused is a virtue that will distinguish excellent people from others in ministry and the marketplace. Start with having a single purpose and pursue it with all your might. According to a Chinese proverb, "If you chase two rabbits, both will escape." **There's power in focus:** it leads to mastery and excellent performances.

Finally, lean on the Holy Spirit. Leaning on your understanding, be it in ministry, business, or employment, will lead to many disappointments and failures. According to the Bible, the Holy Spirit teaches us all things. You need the leading of the Holy Spirit no matter your calling or profession if you want to be excellent. Humans are limited to their natural senses, but the Holy Spirit gives you insight into dimensions beyond the physical world. This is an edge over others and a guarantee of success and excellence. The Holy Spirit can give uncommon ideas and solutions to complex problems in your industry.

Remember that the call to leadership is a call to raise leaders. Therefore, build others with this knowledge of achieving excellence in ministry and the marketplace, even as God guides you.

Show the people around you the possibilities they can create by being dedicated, focused, and submitting to the leadership of the Holy Spirit.

Steps to Building a Culture of Excellence

1. Create Processes and Systems

Be systematic in the ways you handle tasks. Do not do things haphazardly. Document successful processes to replicate them in the future. Create suitable systems of communication with your people. An excellent leader is organized. Systems make work easier and increase productivity. Create a set of rules guiding your daily activities.

2. Grow Your Circle of Influence

Excellent leaders know they cannot do everything by themselves. They need people who believe in them and their dreams and are willing to partner with them.

You must be deliberate and intentional about building your circle of influence as a leader. Find resourceful people who will add value to you and help you in your journey toward excellence. Submit yourself to mentorship from leaders who have achieved what you aim for. Build a team of creative and talented individuals who are passionate and creative. Make friends with ambitious and goal-oriented individuals.

Some ways to grow your influence include: attending conferences, workshops, and seminars, joining communities of your interest, be teachable, and resourceful.

3. Develop Customs and Cultures

Excellent leaders have a collection of values, beliefs, ethics, and behaviors that guide them and the people they work with. Every leader needs to have a unique culture to help them define who they are and what they stand for.

A clearly defined culture attracts the right people who share the same values, tend to be more productive, and enjoy their work.

Organizations with undefined or toxic cultures are at a higher risk of poor performance and results. Employee turnover rates will be high and the work environment will be tense.

4. Have a Mindset Shift

Excellent leadership begins with the mind. How you think and view things determines the way you act, and how you act determines the outcome of your life. Therefore, an excellent leader has an excellent mindset.

You have to see things differently. For example, see challenges as opportunities and focus on process and progress instead of results and perfection. You must also believe that you have all it takes to achieve your dream. Have a "can do" mindset.

5. Commanding

Three things are crucial here: **Activate**, **Impart**, and **Release**.

In my recently published book, *Eikonic Leadership: 8 Qualities That Separate You From The Ordinary*, I discuss the Air concept, activating, imparting, and releasing leaders into their purpose with Excellence.

Excellent leaders *activate* their dreams, plans, goals, and vision. They set it in motion by working hard toward it. They understand that a dream not worked upon is just an idea or imagination.

Next is to *impart*. To impart is to communicate and to bestow something on someone. You need a tribe of people to run with your vision. If it is big enough then you can't do it alone. So, you need people who you will share your vision with. People who are willing to work and partner with you. Break down your big dreams into actionable and measurable steps so they can understand and internalize them.

Finally, *release*. Launch into the marketplace. Impact people and your environment. Be a change maker, trailblazer, blueprint, and template for someone, solve problems, and make things better. Use your gifts, talents, and resources to create opportunities.

6. Challenge the status quo

Average leaders do basic things; extraordinary leaders do extraordinary things. You must be courageous enough to take the road less taken and do what many are afraid of doing.

Be creative and think outside the box because your reward will be greater at the end of the day. Only those who dare to go against the norm write their names in the sands of time.

7. Become a Change Catalyst

To be a change catalyst is to be able to initiate or accelerate change. We live in a changing world where there is a massive shift. An excellent leader shouldn't be caught unawares and must also be flexible to adapt to change in their industry or society. Don't be rigid and slow. Have a vision, engage and empower people to achieve goals.

8. Be Consistent

The journey toward excellent leadership is definitely not a smooth ride. If it was, everyone would be wearing an excellent leader badge. So, it takes a lot of grit, sweat, and blood. It's a painful journey but rewarding.

However, it rewards only those who refuse to back down in the face of fear and challenges. Choose your path, keep going, and don't look back. Keep showing up, maintain the tempo and never slow down. Have a message and idea, keep talking about it, and don't stop working on it. Consistency always pays.

7 Enemies of Excellence

As you pursue excellence as a leader, there are certain things to avoid. The journey toward excellent leadership is that of learning and unlearning. Here are some things that can stop you from becoming an excellent leader.

1. Unhealthy Relationships

Jim Rohn states, "You are the average of the five people you spend most of your time with." Spend your time with achievers and bright minds, and you will become like them; spend time with losers and unserious people and become the latest loser.

Unhealthy relationships are like chains; they limit your movement. To fly higher and become an excellent leader, you must let go of the weight slowing you down.

Cut off from pessimistic people; they always have reasons why your dream is not achievable. Stay away from lazy people; they will kill your passion and drive to aim for more.

Spend time with people who inspire and challenge you, people who have achieved your goals and walked the path you want to journey on.

2. Procrastination

You can't become an excellent leader when you find it hard to focus and complete a task or project. How do you become a great leader when you miss deadlines, perform tasks poorly and consistently fail to deliver results? No one will take you seriously.

Procrastination can be caused by fear of a task, lack of motivation, or sheer laziness—no excuses for failure as a leader. Therefore, you must learn how to manage your time and find ways to get things done.

To avoid procrastination, you must set clear and measurable goals. Also, dismantle every form of fear. Better still, ensure you're well-equipped and skilled for a task before accepting it.

3. Unpreparedness

Success is when preparation meets opportunity. You can't maintain what you are not prepared to have. Only those who have tilled the ground planted and watered enjoy a harvest. It's either you are ready for leadership, or you're not. There's no middle ground.

To be excellent requires a lot of work. First, you must build your body, mind, and soul. You must be physically, mentally, and emotionally fit to be excellent. Taking care of one while neglecting others will not work. Therefore, preparation is not an option; it's a must. Sign up for the gym, study books, attend seminars, take nutrition seriously, build emotional stamina, etc.

4. Perfectionism

Striving for flawlessness and perfection is good, but don't be obsessed with it. We live in an imperfect world where something that seems perfect today would be imperfect tomorrow. However, we all have the opportunity to improve and innovate. Knowing this in your journey toward excellence will give you peace.

Work hard to give your best but don't set unrealistic goals to stress you out. You can continually improve; it's a marathon, not a sprint.

5. Overthinking

Overthinking is dwelling on negative thoughts. It's an unhealthy habit of holding on to the past in your mind and worrying about the future. Overthinking drains your mental and emotional energy, leaving you empty and not feeling any better.

What makes you excellent is strategic thinking and brainstorming for ideas and solutions. Excessive worry and stagnant thinking do not change anything but make you feel worse.

6. Fear

You must take risks, face uncertainty, and try new things to attain excellence in leadership. However, only fear can stop you from trying. Fear prevents you from leaving your comfort zone and facing challenges. Nevertheless, you must conquer new challenges before getting to a new height or level. The more you face your fears, the more you become better, wiser, and stronger.

An unfortunate truth about fear is that most of the things people are afraid of are not real. They are just a figment of imagination. Someone defined fear as false evidence appearing real. It's all in your head. Rise and face it.

7. Self-doubt

Self-doubt is a feeling everyone gets when faced with a new challenge. However, it becomes harmful when it becomes incessant and prolonged, hindering you from taking action.

A lack of faith in oneself characterizes self-doubt. It causes anxiety, depression, and difficulty in making decisions. Self-doubt also makes you feel less qualified for an opportunity, even when you have all it takes to get the job done. It comes with a feeling of inadequacy.

Self-doubt is a major hindrance to achieving excellence. A leader who doesn't trust in himself and his abilities cannot gain the trust and loyalty of others.

One simple way to conquer self-doubt is to know that someone out there with half of your skill, experience, and expertise is achieving more and doing more.

Building Me While I'm Building It is a call to mentorship.

It is a responsibility to raise men and women who will cause visible changes in the marketplace.

Therefore, see yourself as a conduit through which God's blessing and power flow towards your generation, watering them, nurturing them, and helping them grow into maturity and excellence.

On the following pages, I've gifted you with a collection of affirmations. Post them by your nightstand, on your bathroom mirror, or next to your coffeemaker, so as you prepare yourself to conquer your day, you are affirmed to move forward in excellence!

Be blessed!

Affirmations for Your Journey

by Dr. Ansonya L. Pace-Burke

Excellent Leader Affirmations

- I am an exceptional leader; leadership comes naturally to me.

- I am a courageous leader that faces and overcome challenges.

- I am an excellent leader who masters skills and principles.

- I am a relevant leader who prioritizes personal development.

- I am an innovative leader; I birth new ideas never seen before.

- I am a fearless leader; I break protocols and challenge the status quo.

- My mind is a fertile land where fantastic ideas grow.

- I am a kind leader who leads with compassion, love, and understanding.

- I am a consistent leader; I never stop until I reach my goal.

- My energy is contagious; I inspire and motivate.

- I am a change agent; I solve problems and complex challenges.

- I am an outstanding leader because I have an excellent spirit.

- I am an extraordinary leader; people are drawn to me.

- I am an unstoppable leader; I have abundant energy.

- I have all it takes to be a successful leader.

- I am an excellent leader; I have an uncommon insight into situations.

About the Authors

Cedric D. Nesbitt is a relevant leader, SOUL-utionist, visionary, author, and Leadership Architect whose concepts and message transcend cultural, generational, and socio-economic barriers. His passion is to equip, train and activate individuals, transforming potential into measurable purpose. Nesbitt also utilizes his unique and global appeal to partner with the masses in the achievement of personal, relational, and leadership goals.

As an acclaimed author, Nesbitt's commitment is to bring transformation to generations. He has authored multiple book projects but just to name a few: *The 21-Day Reboot Your Life*; *PurposeFULL*; *No More Neutral: The One Thing You Can't Afford to Be Empty Of*; *Soul Ties: Getting Free and Staying Free from Toxic Relationships*; *Cultivate*.

Nesbitt is also the Senior Leader of The PIVOT Place Phoenix & The PIVOT Place Amarillo, thriving apostolic training centers based in Phoenix, Arizona, and Amarillo, Texas. He also is the founder and executive leader of the PIVOT Global Community, an in-person and online community that spans the globe, connected holistically creating opportunities for engagement, education, and empowerment. Nesbitt is also the Lead Apostle of the PIVOT Network, covering churches, hubs, ministry centers, and initiatives in the United States and across the globe.

Through the PIVOT conglomerate, Nesbitt utilizes conferences, empowerment weekends, retreats, and training modules to cultivate and activate individuals across the world.

Nesbitt is married to his best friend and lovely wife, Tyra D. Nesbitt. They are blessed with three sons: Christian Emmanuel York, Nicolas Camden, and Brayden Alexander.

You can find Nesbitt at **www.cedricnesbitt.com**

Maria Mwangi's passion for the Event Industry went from a hobby and side business to a full career change in entrepreneurship after the housing crisis of 2008. Mrs. Mwangi started as a wedding planner, Director of Catering, and corporate planner for large-scale events. After years of success, she has become a City, State, and International Award-Winning Event

ABOUT THE AUTHORS

Producer. In addition, several of her events and styled shoots have been published online and in print as well as featured on the cover of a magazine.

Mrs. Mwangi feels most blessed and full of gratitude because she has been honored to see her clients through the most intimate parts of their lives. She is currently the Director of Sales and Events for Warehouse215, one of the largest historic event venues in the downtown Phoenix warehouse district.

Maria Mwangi co-authored her first book, *Conceived by Grace: A No Fear, Faith-filled Pregnancy Journal for Those who have Experienced Infertility, Miscarriage, and Infant Loss*. After suffering three miscarriages (losing three angel babies), Maria and her late husband, Kenneth Mwangi, became proud parents of two boys. Now two young men ages 16 & 14.

Mrs. Mwangi decided to attribute to the *Building Me While I'm Building It* project because she felt it was time to share her testimony of finding God's grace and peace after losing her husband. She hopes to inspire and encourage other widowers out there struggling to juggle kids, careers, and life without their partner.

Char-Michelle McDowell, a native of Chicago, Illinois, inhales the air of purpose and exhales the breath of encouragement, empowerment, and enrichment to help individuals live a fulfilling life, with a focused approach. She does this through facilitating workshops, writing books, and curriculum programming.

This woman of faith has overcome and mentored those dealing with rejection, low esteem, and a lack of confidence. With over 20 years of serving in leadership, she lives life as she was designed to lead it as an Author, Certified Enrichment Coach, Process Consultant, Licensed Minister, International Speaker, and Transformational Leader.

Char loves to read, watch movies, laugh, and hang out with family and friends. Her mantra is "Don't live to exist. Lead to live!

Char-Michelle is available for: Professional & Ministry Conferences; Leadership Development Training; Consulting or Coaching Services. Her first work, *Just B.E.E It*, is available on Amazon.

Please submit requests via her website: www.leadwithchar.comor email at **info@leadwithchar.com**

Shyla Bassey epitomizes integrity, a strong work ethic, resilience, and creativity in every facet of her real estate career. Her single-minded focus paired with superior client skills result in high-quality experiences that are as impactful as they are memorable. It is with great professionalism and determination that Shyla partners up with her clients, assisting them in one of the most important investments of their lives. Shyla is a graduate of Arizona State University where she received her BA in Business & Communications. She developed early on, an unwavering dedication to excellence, which has connected her with leaders in her field to form a team of professionals in addition to a vast network comprised of real estate attorneys, appraisers, and lenders, among others. She holds 12 years of experience in banking having managed large teams and successfully increased customer satisfaction across regions.

Above all, Shyla attributes her belief that "I can do all things through Christ" as the determining catalyst in propelling her forward in her career goals and entrepreneurial endeavors. Outside of real estate, Shyla enjoys spending quality time with her family & friends, trying new restaurants across the Phoenix valley, and traveling the world. Her sole mission is to be the best so she can best serve her clients and leave a legacy for her family. *Building Me While I'm Building It* is her first book project.

Jaquay Reed is a Tech Industry leader in the corporate world with over 17 years of experience.

Her passion is caring for young children. Over the past 7 years, she has served in the nursery and pre-k in the children's ministry at her church. Her passion for youth ministries led her to launch her first start-up, **Nothing But Love Childcare, LLC** in 2020. After gaining her footing in entrepreneurship, she launched **For Girls Of Destiny** in 2022, a ministry for young girls.

She didn't know if she could, but she did it! Her chapter regarding humility is exactly what she embraced to write her first-ever published work. Jaquay practices her walk in humility by doing the works that please God. This has trickled over into her social life with family and friends, work life as an IT Support Lead Technician, and as a Director in youth ministries. It's her service to others that keep her smiling and full of joy.

To stay connected with Jaquay, follow her on Instagram, **@J.Reed**, where she shares her love for great food, travel, hiking, and her faith journey.

Robin K. Butler is the Founder and CEO of Catalyst Consulting Agency, LLC, a personal and professional development consultancy, where she helps her clients gain their spark to "LEAD" **L**(earn) **E**(enrich) **A**(spire) **D**(iscover) their passion, purpose, and potential. This is done through her Catalyst 4C (Foresee) Model which includes **Coaching, Conversations, Courses, and Consulting** with individuals and organizations. She is an international speaker with a passion for emotional intelligence and conflict resolution leading to her unique approach to the facilitation of team building and as a diversity and culture champion. Her mission is to help her corporate and faith-based clients as well as colleagues effectively communicate, enhance connection, encourage collaboration, and ebb conflict.

Robin has a BS in Business Management, MA in Organizational Management, and is pursuing a Doctor of Management in Organizational Leadership. Robin is an Executive Program Consultant as well as a Certified Maxwell Leadership Coach, Speaker, and Facilitator.

Robin is the wife of Timothy L. Butler, the mother of Andrea Brielle Wright (Chris), and the proud Gigi to Kai Parker. She enjoys sharing her faith and belief in God that all things are possible with Him.

Tiffany Hodgest is an emerging leader and prophetic voice to the nations, currently serving as leader of the Intercessory Team for Pivot Global Network under the leadership of Apostle Cedric and Tyra Nesbitt. God has called her to teach, train, develop, and activate intercessors. She has a military stance concerning prayer and spiritual warfare. She is also widely sought out by corporations because of her ability to lead and manage people.

Growing up, Tiffany struggled with abandonment issues, depression, and trauma, which led to her attempted suicide. But God intervened, surrounding her with a tenacious woman of God, her former co-pastor, and her mother's loving support and strength. These experiences exposed her to the importance of women in leadership.

Tiffany never explored higher education to land leadership roles in the marketplace but was content with playing her part on teams. However, the strength of will she carried with her from such strong women role models quickly showed in the workplace, causing her to be sought out for management positions. She quickly found being a manager a good fit, and that God opened those doors when she needed them most. In the marketplace, as well as in church, she's needed to wear many hats and has met each challenge as an opportunity to expand and grow.

Some time ago, God began to provoke Tiffany to write about divine expansion in her life to inspire others. Not long after, she was invited to write for *Building Me While I'm Building It*, and immediately knew God was in the details. Tiffany hopes to continue writing and is looking to write a prayer book in the near future.

Dr. Ansonya L. Pace-Burke is an internationally certified chaplain, life coach, intercessor, entrepreneur, and visionary

ABOUT THE AUTHORS

leader. She has an apostolic grace to bring divine order, a disruptive anointing to lead change and speak truth to power, and a call to activate, impart, and release God's wisdom with authority. She believes God deserves our very best in everything that we do, and she uses her God-given gifts to encourage others to seek a personal, minute-by-minute relationship with their Lord and Savior. Dr. Burke is passionate about empowering all types of leaders to confidently and boldly walk out their unique assignments within the marketplace, ministry, and academia.

Dr. Burke has a Bachelor's in Family Studies and Counseling from the University of Arizona, a Master's in Organizational Management from the University of Phoenix, and received her Ph.D. in Advanced Clinical Chaplaincy & Christian Pastoral Psychotherapy from Heart Bible Institute International in 2022.

She is the proud mother of two children—Master Quentin and Princess Aniyah Burke.

Dr. Burke's breakout work, *Eikonic Leadership: Eight Qualities that Separate you from the Ordinary*, was released in April 2019. Her prayer challenge journal, *Speak It Until You See It: 31 Days of Declaring & Decreeing God's Word Over Your Life* is currently available in paperback and kindle unlimited.

You can find Dr. Burke at **www.ansonyaburke.com**.

1. Burke, Ansonya. 2019. Eikonic Leadership: 8 Unique Qualities That Separate You from the Ordinary. San Antonio: Principles In Action Consulting LLC.
2. Burke, Ansonya. 2019. Eikonic Leadership: 8 Unique Qualities That Separate You from the Ordinary. San Antonio: Principles In Action Consulting LLC.
3. Colbert, Evangeline. 2016. Live to Win!: 5 Essentials for Your Victory and Success. iHope Publishing.
4. BrainyQuote.com. 2022. "Dale Carnegie Quotes." Accessed September 9, 2022. https://www.brainyquote.com/quotes/dale_carnegie_132157
5. McDowell, C. (2020). Just B.E.E. IT! Bloomington, IL: Independently Published.
6. Merriam-Webster.com Dictionary, s.v. "confidence," accessed September 9, 2022, https://www.merriam-webster.com/dictionary/confidence.
7. King James Bible, Luke 1:38
8. New King James Bible Joshua 1:8
9. McDowell 2020, 77-78
10. Barnum, P. (2020). "Five Benefits of Self-Confidence." Accessed September 9, 2022. https://pamelabarnum.com/five-benefits-of-self-confidence/
11. John 13:12-17 (TPT); Galatians 5:13 (NLT/MSG/NIV)
12. James 3:13 (NLT)
13. New International Version (NIV), Proverbs 3:5-6.

14. "influence ." The Oxford Pocket Dictionary of Current English. Encyclopedia.com. (August 25, 2022). https://www.encyclopedia.com/humanities/dictionaries-thesauruses-pictures-and-press-releases/influence
15. Merriam-Webster.com Dictionary, s.v. "expand," accessed September 9, 2022, https://www.merriam-webster.com/dictionary/expand.
16. Merriam-Webster.com Dictionary, s.v. "expansion," accessed September 9, 2022, https://www.merriam-webster.com/dictionary/expansion.

Made in the USA
Columbia, SC
07 February 2023